Endangered Species

Endangered Species

VOLUME 1
Mammals

Rob Nagel

U·X·L®
AN IMPRINT OF GALE

DETROIT • LONDON

Endangered Species
Rob Nagel

STAFF

Julie L. Carnagie, *U•X•L Developmental Editor*
Sonia Benson, *U•X•L Senior Developmental Editor*
Carol DeKane Nagel, *U•X•L Managing Editor*
Thomas L. Romig, *U•X•L Publisher*

Mary Beth Trimper, *Production Director*
Evi Seoud, *Production Manager*
Shanna Heilveil, *Production Associate*

Cynthia Baldwin, *Product Design Manager*
Barbara J. Yarrow, *Graphic Services Supervisor*
Michelle DiMercurio, *Art Director*

Margaret Chamberlain, *Permissions Specialist*
Jessica L. Ulrich, *Permissions Associate*

Library of Congress Cataloging-in-Publication Data
Nagel, Rob.
      Endangered Species / Rob Nagel
        p.   cm.
      Includes bibliographical references and index.
      Contents: v. 1. Mammals — v. 2. Arachnids, birds, crustaceans, insects, and mollusks — v. 3.
Amphibians, fish, plants, and reptiles.
      Summary: Entries on 200 extinct, endangered, vulnerable, and threatened animals and plants
describe the individual species, its habitat and current distribution, and efforts to protect and preserve it.
      ISBN 0-7876-1875-6 (set: hardcover). — ISBN 0-7876-1876-4 (vol. 1). — ISBN
0-7876-1877-2 (vol. 2). — ISBN 0-7876-1878-0 (vol. 3)
      1. Endangered species—Juvenile literature [1. Endangered species—Encyclopedias.] I. Title.
QL83.N3546   1998
333.95'42—cd21   98-34259
                                                                                            CIP

###

Contents

VOLUME 2: Arachnids, Birds, Crustaceans, Insects, and Mollusks

VOLUME 3: Amphibians, Fish, Plants, and Reptiles

Reader's Guide

Endangered Species presents information on endangered and threatened mammals, birds, reptiles, amphibians, fish, mollusks, insects, arachnids, crustaceans, and plants. Its two hundred entries were chosen to give a glimpse of the broad range of species currently facing endangerment. While well–publicized examples such as the American bison, northern spotted owl, and gray wolf are examined, so, too, are less conspicuous—yet no less threatened—species such as the Australian ant, Cape vulture, and Peebles Navajo cactus.

The entries are spread across three volumes and are divided into sections by classes. Within each class, species are arranged alphabetically by common name.

Each entry begins with the species's common and scientific names. A fact box containing classification information—phylum (or division), class, order, and family—for that species follows. The box also lists the current status of the species in the wild according to the International Union for Conservation of Nature (IUCN) and Natural Resources and the U.S. Fish and Wildlife Service (which administers the Endangered Species Act). Finally, the box lists the country or countries where the species currently ranges.

Locator maps outlining the range of a particular species are included in each entry to help users find unfamiliar countries or locations. In most entries, a color or black–and–white photo provides a more concrete visualization of the species. Sidebar boxes containing interesting and related information are also included in some entries.

Each entry is broken into three sections:

- The information under the subhead **Description and Biology** provides a general description of the species. This includes physical dimensions, eating and reproductive habits, and social behavior.

- The information under the subhead **Habitat and Current Distribution** describes where the species is found, its preferred habitat, and, if available, recent estimates of its population size.

- The information under the subhead **History and Conservation Measures** relates, if possible, the history of the species and the factors currently threatening it. Conservation efforts to save the species, if any are underway, are also described.

Beginning each volume of *Endangered Species* is an overview of the history and current state of endangerment and its causes and a discussion of the International Union for Conservation of Nature and Natural Resources (IUCN–The World Conservation Union) that includes a brief history of the organization, its current focus, and a brief explanation of the status categories in which the IUCN places imperiled species. The final section focuses on the Endangered Species Act, briefly examining its passage, purpose, implementation, status categories, and current state.

Each volume ends with a further research section composed of books, periodicals, internet addresses, and environmental organizations. The book listing is annotated. The environmental organizations list—a selected catalog of organizations focusing on endangered species—contains mailing addresses, telephone numbers, internet addresses (if available), and a brief description of each organization.

Finally, the volumes conclude with a cumulative index providing access to all the species discussed throughout *Endangered Species*.

The scope of this work is neither definitive nor exhaustive. No work on this subject can be. The information presented is as current as possible, but the state of endangered species, sadly, changes almost daily.

Acknowledgments

Special thanks are due for the invaluable comments and suggestions provided by the *Endangered Species* advisors:

Valerie Doud, Science Teacher, Peru Junior High School, Peru Indiana

Melba Holland, Earth Science/Science Department Head, Slaton Junior High School, Slaton, Texas

Bonnie L. Raasch, Media Specialist, C. B. Vernon Middle School, Marion, Iowa

The editors of *Endangered Species* also graciously thank Tom Romig and Julie Carnagie for their commitment to this project and for their patience and understanding during its completion. It is a continuing privilege and pleasure to work with the U•X•L family.

A special note of thanks goes out to Karen D'Angelo—Advanced Master Gardener, sister, and friend—for her generous assistance with early research and her occasional explication of scientific matters throughout the project. Her knowledge of the natural world is matched only by her concern for it.

Comments and Suggestions

We welcome your comments on *Endangered Species* and suggestions for species to be included in future editions of *Endangered Species*. Please write: Editors, *Endangered Species*, U•X•L, 27500 Drake Rd., Farmington Hills, Michigan 48331–3535; call toll free: 1–800–877–4253; or fax: 248–699–8066.

Endangerment and Its Causes: An Overview

Living organisms have been disappearing from the face of Earth since the beginning of life on the planet. Most of the species that have ever lived on Earth are now extinct. Extinction and endangerment can occur naturally as a normal process in the course of evolution. It can be the result of a catastrophic event, such as the collision of an asteroid with Earth. Scientists believe an asteroid stuck the planet off Mexico's Yucatán Peninsula some 65,000,000 years ago, bringing about the extinction of almost 50 percent of the plant species and 75 percent of the animal species then living on Earth, including the dinosaurs. Wide–spread climate changes, disease, and competition among species can also result in natural extinction. To date, scientists believe there have been five great natural extinction episodes in Earth's history.

Since humans became the dominant species on the planet, however, the rate at which other species have become extinct has increased dramatically. Especially since the seventeenth century, technological advances and an ever–expanding human population have changed the natural world as never before. At present, scientists believe extinctions caused by humans are taking place at 100 to 1,000 times nature's normal rate between great extinction episodes. Species are disappearing faster than they can be created through evolution.

It is impossible to measure the total number of species endangered or going extinct because scientists have described and named only a small percentage of Earth's species. Just 1,400,000 species—out an estimated 10,000,000 to 100,000,000—have been described to date.

Scientists do know that humans are endangering species and the natural world primarily in three ways: habitat destruction, commercial exploitation of animals and plants, and the transplantation of species from one part of the world to another.

Habitat destruction

The destruction of habitats all over the world is the primary reason species are becoming extinct or endangered. Houses, highways, dams, industrial buildings, and ever–spreading farms now dominate landscapes formerly occupied by forests, prairies, deserts, scrublands, and wetlands. Since the beginning of European settlement in America, over 65,000,000 acres of wetlands have been drained. One million acres alone vanished between 1985 and 1995.

Habitat destruction can be obvious or it can be subtle, occurring over a long period of time without being noticed. Pollution, such as sewage from cities and chemical runoff from farms, can change the quality and quantity of water in streams and rivers. To species living in a delicately balanced habitat, this disturbance can be as fatal as the clear–cutting of a rain forest.

As remaining habitats are carved into smaller and smaller pockets or islands, remaining species are forced to exist in these crowded areas, which causes further habitat destruction. These species become less adaptable to environmental change; they become more vulnerable to extinction. Scientists believe that when a habitat is cut by 90 percent, one–half of its plants, animals, insects, and microscopic life–forms will become extinct.

Commercial exploitation

Animals have been hunted by humans not only for their meat but for parts of their bodies that are used to create medicines, love potions, and trinkets. Overhunting has caused the extinction of many species and brought a great many others to the brink of extinction. Examples include species of whales, slaughtered for their oil and baleen. The rhinoceroses of Africa are critically endangered, having been killed mainly for their horns.

International treaties outlaw the capture and trade of many endangered or threatened species. These laws, however, are difficult to enforce. The smuggling of endangered species is a huge business. In 1996, between $10,000,000,000 and $20,000,000,000 in plants and animals were traded illegally around the world.

Introduced species

Native species are those that have inhabited a given biological landscape for a long period of time. They have adapted to the environment, climate, and other species in that locale. Introduced or exotic species are those that have been brought into that landscape by humans, either accidentally or intentionally.

In some cases, these introduced species may not cause any harm. They may, over time, adapt to their new surroundings and fellow species, becoming "native." Most often, however, introduced species seriously disrupt ecological balances. They compete with native species for food and shelter. Often, they prey on the native species, who lack natural defenses against the intruders. In the last 500 years, introduced insects, cats, pigs, rats, and others have caused the endangerment or outright extinction of hundreds of native species.

Endangered Species Fact Boxes and Classification: An Explanation

Each entry in *Endangered Species* begins with the common name of a species, followed by its scientific name. Underneath is a shaded fact box. This box contains the classification information for that species: phylum (or division), class, order, and family. It also lists the current status of that species in the wild according to the International Union for Conservation of Nature and Natural Resources (IUCN; see p. xxiii) and the Endangered Species List compiled under the Endangered Species Act (ESA; see p. xxv). Finally, the box lists the country or countries where the species is currently found and provides a locator map for the range of the species.

Classification

Biological classification, or taxonomy, is the system of arranging plants and animals in groups according to their similarities. This system, which scientists around the world currently use, was developed by eighteenth–century Swedish botanist (a person specializing in the study of plants) Carolus Linnaeus. Linnaeus created a multilevel system or pyramid-like structure of nomenclature (naming) in which living organisms were grouped according to the number of physical traits they had in common. The ranking of the system, going from general to specific, is kingdom, phylum (or division for plants), class, order, and family. The more specific the level (closer to the top of the pyramid), the more traits shared by the organisms placed in that level.

Scientists currently recognize five kingdoms of organisms: Animalia (animals, fish, humans); Plantae (plants, trees, grasses); Fungi (mushrooms, lichens); Protista (bacteria, certain algae, other one–celled organisms having nuclei); and Monera (bacteria, blue–green algae, other one–celled organisms without nuclei).

Every living organism is placed into one of these kingdoms. Organisms within kingdoms are then divided into phylums (or divisions for plants) based on distinct and defining characteristics. An example would be the phylum Chordata, which contains all the members of the kingdom Animalia that have a backbone. Organisms in a specific phylum or division are then further divided into classes based on more distinct and defining characteristics. The dividing continues on through orders and then into families, where most organisms probably have the same behavioral patterns.

To further define an organism, Linnaeus also developed a two–part naming system—called binomial nomenclature—in which each living organism was given a two–part Latin name to distinguish it from other members in its family. The first name—italicized and capitalized—is the genus of the organism. The second name—italicized but not capitalized—is its species. This species name is an adjective, usually descriptive or geographic. Together, the genus and species form an organism's scientific name.

How similar organisms are separated by their scientific names can be seen in the example of the white oak and the red oak. All oak trees belong to the genus *Quercus*. The scientific name of white oak is *Quercus alba* (*alba* is Latin for "white"), while that of the red oak is *Quercus rubra* (*rubra* is Latin for "red").

Since each species or organism has only one name under binomial nomenclature, scientists worldwide who do not speak the same languages are able to communicate with each other about species.

International Union for Conservation of Nature and Natural Resources (IUCN–The World Conservation Union)

The IUCN is one of the world's oldest international conservation organizations. It was established in Fountainbleau, France, on October 5, 1947. It is a worldwide alliance of governments, government agencies, and nongovernmental organizations. Working with scientists and experts, the IUCN tries to encourage and assist nations and societies around the world to conserve nature and to use natural resources wisely. At present, IUCN members represent 74 governments, 105 government agencies, and more than 700 nongovernmental organizations.

The IUCN has six volunteer commissions. The largest and most active of these is the Species Survival Commission (SSC). The mission of the SSC is to conserve biological diversity by developing programs that help save, restore, and manage species and their habitats. One of the many activities of the SSC is the production of the *IUCN Red List of Threatened Animals* and the *IUCN Red List of Threatened Plants*.

These publications, which have provided the foundation for *Endangered Species*, present scientifically based information on the status of threatened species around the world. Species are classified according to their existence in the wild and the current threats to that existence. The categories differ slightly between animals and plants.

IUCN Red List categories

The *IUCN Red List of Threatened Animals* places threatened animals into one of nine categories:

- **Extinct:** A species that no longer exists anywhere around the world.

- **Extinct in the wild:** A species that no longer exists in the wild, but exists in captivity or in an area well outside its natural range.

- **Critically endangered:** A species that is facing an extremely high risk of extinction in the wild in the immediate future.

- **Endangered:** A species that is facing a high risk of extinction in the wild in the near future.

- **Vulnerable:** A species that is facing a high risk of extinction in the wild in the medium–term future.

- **Lower risk: Conservation dependent:** A species that is currently the focus of a conservation program. If the program is halted, the species would suffer and would qualify for one of the threatened categories above within a period of five years.

- **Lower risk: Near threatened:** A species that does not qualify for Conservation Dependent status, but is close to qualifying for Vulnerable status.

- **Lower risk: Least concern:** A species that qualifies for neither Conservation Dependent status or Near Threatened status.

- **Data deficient:** A species on which there is little information to assess its risk of extinction. Because of the possibility that future research will place the species in a threatened category, more information is required.

The *IUCN Red List of Threatened Plants* places threatened plants into one of six categories:

- **Extinct:** A species that no longer exists anywhere around the world.

- **Extinct/Endangered:** A species that is considered possibly to be extinct in the wild.

- **Endangered:** A species that is in immediate danger of extinction if the factors threatening it continue.

- **Vulnerable:** A species that will likely become endangered if the factors threatening it continue.

- **Rare:** A species with a small world population that is currently neither endangered nor threatened, but is at risk.

- **Indeterminate:** A species that is threatened, but on which there is not enough information to place it in the appropriate category of Extinct, Endangered, Vulnerable, or Rare.

Endangered Species Act

The Endangered Species Act (ESA) was passed by the U.S. Congress in 1973 and was reauthorized in 1988. The purpose of the ESA is to recover species around the world that are in danger of human–caused extinction. Through the creation of a list of endangered animals and plants (the Endangered Species List), the act seeks to provide a means of conserving those species and their ecosystems.

The U.S. Fish and Wildlife Service (USFWS), a part of the Department of Interior, is the federal agency responsible for listing (or reclassifying or delisting) endangered and threatened species on the Endangered Species List. The decision to list a species is based solely on scientific factors. Once a species is placed on the list, the USFWS is required to develop a plan for its recovery. The USFWS also makes sure that any actions by the U.S. government or citizens do not further harm the listed species. However, the ESA explicitly requires the balancing of species protection with economic development.

Species are placed on the list in one of two categories:

- **Endangered:** A species that is in danger of extinction throughout all or a significant part of its range.
- **Threatened:** A species that is likely to become endangered in the foreseeable future.

The ESA outlaws the buying, selling, transporting, importing, or exporting of any listed species. Most important, the act bans the taking of any listed species within the United States and its territorial seas. "Taking" is defined as harassing, harming, pursuing, hunting, shooting, wounding, cutting, trapping, killing, removing, capturing, or collecting. The taking of listed species is prohibited on both private and public lands.

Violators of the ESA are subject to heavy fines. Individuals can face up to $100,000 in fines and up to one year's imprisonment. Organizations found in violation of the act may be fined up to $200,000.

As of the beginning of 1998, there were 1,126 species on the Endangered Species List. This total included 458 animals and 668 plants. The majority of species on the list—896—were placed in the Endangered category.

There has been much criticism of the ESA since its passage. Opponents of the act believe it prohibits human activity and progress. They believe it places the rights of humans behind those of other species. The debate over these supposed aspects of the ESA will likely continue.

What is not debatable, however, is the fact that the ESA has worked to save endangered species. Of the 128 U.S. species that were on the Endangered Species List when the ESA was passed in 1973, almost 60 percent have recovered, are improving, or are in stable condition.

Words to Know

A

Alpine: Relating to mountainous regions.

Arid: Land that receives less than 10 inches (250 millimeters) of rainfall annually and has a high rate of evaporation.

B

Biodiversity: The entire variety of life on Earth.

Brackish: A mixture of freshwater and saltwater; briny water.

C

Canopy: The uppermost spreading branchy layer of a forest.

Carapace: A shell or bony covering on the back of animals such as turtles, lobsters, crabs, and armadillos.

Carnivore: An animal that eats mainly meat.

Carrion: Dead and decaying flesh.

Cetacean: An aquatic mammal that belongs to the order Cetacea, which includes whales, dolphins, and porpoises.

CITES: Abbreviation for Convention on International Trade in Endangered Species of Wild Fauna and Flora; an international agreement by 143 nations to prohibit trade of endangered wildlife.

Clear–cutting: The process of cutting down all the trees in a forest area.

Clutch: The number of eggs produced or incubated at one time.

Competitor: A species that may compete for the same resources as another species.

Conservation: The management and protection of the natural world.

D

Deforestation: The loss of forests as they are rapidly cut down to produce timber or to make land available for agriculture.

Desertification: The gradual transformation of productive land into that with desertlike conditions.

Diurnal: Active during the day.

Domesticated: Animals trained to live with or be of use to humans.

E

Ecosystem: An ecological community, including plants, animals, and microorganisms, considered together with their environment.

Endangered: Species in danger of extinction in the foreseeable future.

Endangered Species Act (ESA): The legislation, passed by the U.S. Congress in 1973, which protects listed species.

Endangered Species List: The list of species protected under the Endangered Species Act.

Estuary: The place where freshwater enters the sea (e.g., at a river mouth).

Extinction: A species or subspecies is extinct when no living members exist.

F

Fauna: The animal life of a particular region, geological period, or environment.

Feral: An animal that has escaped from domestication and has become wild.

Fledge: When birds grow the feathers needed for flight.

Flora: The plants of a particular region, geological period, or environment.

G

Gestation: Pregnancy.

H

Habitat: The environment in which specified organisms live.

Herbivore: An animal that eats mainly plants.

I

Introduced species: Flora or fauna not native to an area, but introduced from a different ecosystem.

IUCN: Abbreviation for International Union for the Conservation of Nature and Natural Resources; publishes *IUCN Red List of Threatened Animals* and *IUCN Red List of Threatened Plants.*

L

Larval: The immature stage of certain insects and animals, usually of a species that develops by complete metamorphosis.

Lichen: A plantlike composite consisting of a fungus and an alga.

M

Marsupial: Mammals, such as the kangaroo and the opossum, whose young continue to develop after birth in a pouch on the outside of the mother's body.

Metamorphosis: A change in the form and habits of an animal during natural development.

Migrating: The act of changing location periodically, usually moving seasonally from one region to another.

Molting: The process of shedding an outer covering, such as skin or feathers, for replacement by a new growth.

N

Native species: The flora or fauna indigenous or native to an ecosystem, as opposed to introduced species.

Nocturnal: Most active at night.

O

Old–growth forest: A mature forest dominated by long–lived species (at least 200 years old), but also including younger trees; its complex physical structure includes multiple layers in the canopy, many large trees, and many large dead standing trees and dead logs.

P

Perennial: A plant that lives, grows, flowers, and produces seeds for three or more continuous years.

Prehensile: Adapted for grasping or holding, especially by wrapping around something.

Poaching: Illegally taking protected animals or plants.

Pollution: The contamination of air, water, or soil by the discharge of harmful substances.

Population: A group of organisms of one species occupying a defined area and usually isolated from similar groups of the same species.

Predator: An animal that preys on others.

Pupal: An intermediate, inactive stage between the larva and adult stages in the life cycle of many insects.

R

Rain forest: A dense evergreen forest with an annual rainfall of at least 100 inches (254 cm); may be tropical (e.g., Amazon) or temperate (e.g., Pacific Northwest).

Range: The area naturally occupied by a species.

Reintroduction: The act of placing members of a species in their original habitat.

Reserve: An area of land set aside for the use or protection of a species or group of species.

S

Savanna: A flat, treeless tropical or subtropical grassland.

Scrub: A tract of land covered with stunted or scraggly trees and shrubs.

Slash–and–burn agriculture: The process whereby a forest is cut down and all trees and vegetation are burned to create cleared land.

Species: A group of individuals related by descent and able to breed among themselves but not with other organisms.

Steppe: Vast, semiarid grass–covered plains found in southeast Europe, Siberia, and central North America.

Subspecies: A population of a species distinguished from other such populations by certain characteristics.

Succulent: A plant that has thick, fleshy, water–storing leaves or stems.

T

Taproot: The main root of a plant growing straight downward from the stem.

Territoriality: The behavior displayed by an individual animal, a mating pair, or a group in vigorously defending its domain against intruders.

Tropical: Characteristic of a region or climate that is frost free with temperatures high enough to support—with adequate precipitation—plant growth year round.

Tundra: A relatively flat, treeless plain in alpine, arctic, and antarctic regions.

U

Underbrush: Small trees, shrubs, or similar plants growing on the forest floor underneath taller trees.

U.S. Fish and Wildlife Service: A federal agency that oversees implementation of the Endangered Species Act.

V

Vulnerable: A species is vulnerable when it satisfies some risk criteria, but not at a level that warrants its identification as Endangered.

W

Wetland: A permanently moist lowland area such as a marsh or a swamp.

Endangered Species

ADDAX
Addax nasomaculatus

PHYLUM: Chordata
CLASS: Mammalia
ORDER: Artiodactyla
FAMILY: Bovidae
STATUS: Endangered, IUCN
RANGE: Chad, Mali, Mauritania, Niger

Addax

Addax nasomaculatus

Description and biology

The addax is a large antelope whose coat is gray–brown in winter and almost white in summer. Black hair sprouts from its forehead and from the end of its 10– to 14–inch (25– to 36–centimeters) tail. Two long, thin, spiral horns (each twisting two or three times) extend up and back from the front of the animal's head. An average addax measures about 5 feet (1.5 meters) in length and about 3 feet (1 meter) in height at its shoulder. It weighs between 132 and 287 pounds (60 and 130 kilograms). A female addax usually gives birth to one infant after a gestation (pregnancy) period of eight to nine months.

The addax is at home in a desert environment. It receives all the water it needs from the plants it eats. With its long stride and splayed (spread apart) hooves, the animal easily crosses vast sandy areas in search of sparse desert vegetation. Addax usually travel at night in groups of 5 to 20.

Habitat and current distribution

No more than a few hundred addax—possibly less—currently survive in the wild. These are found in Africa in northeastern Niger, northern Chad, and along the border between Mauritania and Mali.

History and conservation measures

Addax once ranged in Africa from Western Sahara and Mauritania to Egypt and Sudan. Ancient Egyptians domesticated the slow and tame animals. These very traits have led to the animals' present–day decline, as hunters easily capture addax for their prized meat and hide. Despite laws protecting the animals, hunting remains a threat. Additional perils currently facing the addax include drought and tourists who destroy addax habitat with their vehicles while tracking and chasing the animals.

In Niger, the 4,943–square–mile (12,810–square–kilometer) Aïr and Ténère National Nature Reserve provides a large protected habitat for addax. Tourism and other human activities are prohibited within the clearly marked park boundaries. Although addax have existed in this area for centuries, their current population is very low. In the early 1990s, political disputes delayed the reintroduction into the reserve of 50 to 75 addax that had been bred in captivity. More than 1,000 addax are currently held in captivity in the United States, Europe, and the Middle East.

ANTEATER, GIANT
Myrmecophaga tridactyla

PHYLUM: Chordata
CLASS: Mammalia
ORDER: Edentata
FAMILY: Myrmecophagidae
STATUS: Vulnerable, IUCN
RANGE: Argentina, Belize, Bolivia, Brazil, Colombia, Costa Rica, Ecuador, French Guiana, Guatemala, Guyana, Honduras, Nicaragua, Panama, Paraguay, Peru, Suriname, Uruguay, Venezuela

Anteater, giant
Myrmecophaga tridactyla

Description and biology

Coarse, shaggy gray hair covers the giant anteater's long, narrow body. A black and silver–white stripe extends across its shoulders and down its back. The giant anteater's neck and head taper to its distinctive long, cylindrical snout. The animal's eyes and ears are small. Its saliva–coated tongue, used to pluck prey from nests, can extend almost 24 inches (61 centimeters). Its powerful front legs and claws allow the animal to break into termite and ant colonies easily, and also provide a means of defense against predators such as pumas and jaguars. An average giant anteater measures 40 to 50 inches (101 to 127 centimeters) from its head to the end of its body and weighs between 40 and 85 pounds (18 and 38 kilograms). Its shaggy tail can reach from 26 to 35 inches (66 to 89 centimeters) long.

The giant anteater's home range may extend from 1 to 9.6 square miles (2.6 to 24.9 square kilometers). A single giant anteater exists by itself in the wild and comes in contact with other giant anteaters only to mate. A female giant anteater gives birth to a single infant after a 190–day gestation (pregnancy) period. The infant, which rides on the mother's back and nurses for the first six weeks, stays with the mother for more than a year.

Habitat and current distribution

Although the habitat of giant anteaters extends from Guatemala in Central America to Uruguay in South America, scientists believe these animals are almost extinct over much of this great range. The primary reason is habitat destruction, especially of tropical rain forests.

Although sometimes killed for its meat and claws, the giant anteater's tail is also highly prized by hunters.

History and conservation measures

Giant anteaters are killed for their meat, for their claws and tails (which are highly prized), and because people wrongly believe they attack dogs, cattle, and humans. The greatest threat to these animals, however, is fire. During dry seasons, large fires sweep through much of central South America. Farmers also set forest fires in order to increase grazing land for their livestock—what is called slash–and–burn agriculture. While almost all other animals escape these fires by running or flying, giant anteaters usually do not. They are slow–moving and their long hair burns easily.

Giant anteaters are protected from hunters in a number of national parks and nature reserves throughout their vast habitat. In Brazil alone, ten parks and three reserves provide safe haven for the animals. Nonetheless, natural and man–made fires recognize no boundaries, so many giant anteaters have burned to death in protected areas.

ARMADILLO, GIANT
Priodontes maximus:

PHYLUM: Chordata

CLASS: Mammalia

ORDER: Edentata

FAMILY: Dasypodidae

STATUS: Endangered, IUCN
Endangered, ESA

RANGE: Argentina, Bolivia, Brazil, Colombia, Ecuador, French Guiana, Guyana, Paraguay, Peru, Suriname, Uruguay, Venezuela

Armadillo, giant

Priodontes maximus

Description and biology

The giant armadillo is the largest member of the armadillo family, which is composed of twenty–one species. Eleven to thirteen moveable bony plates cover a giant armadillo's back, and three to four flexible bands cover its neck. Its body is dark brown, while its head, tail, and a stripe around the bottom of its shell are whitish. A giant armadillo measures 30 to 39 inches (76 to 99 centimeters) from the tip of its nose to the end of its body. Its tail is about 20 inches (50 centimeters) long. It weighs between 44 and 88 pounds (20 and 40 kilograms).

Unlike certain members of the armadillo family, the giant armadillo cannot roll into a ball, protected by its body armor. To escape from danger, the giant armadillo quickly digs itself into the ground using the long claws on its front legs. The

Giant armadillos are not able to roll themselves into a ball like other members of the armadillo family.

animal also uses these claws to dig for ants, termites, worms, spiders, and other insects which it feeds on at night.

The gestation (pregnancy) period of a female giant armadillo is about four months. She gives birth to one or two infants at a time, each weighing about 4 ounces (113 grams), and they nurse for four to six weeks. The life span of a giant armadillo is 12 to 15 years.

Habitat and current distribution

The giant armadillo is found in many South American countries, from Venezuela and Guyana south to Argentina. However, its primary habitat is the Amazonian rain forest.

History and conservation measures

Hunting, human settlement, and agricultural development have all contributed to the giant armadillo's decline. Although laws in Argentina, Brazil, Colombia, Paraguay, Peru, and Suriname protect the animal, it is still hunted for food in some areas. Of greater concern is the destruction of its habitat, as large areas of rain forest are cleared for homes and farms.

National parks and nature reserves in Brazil, Colombia, Peru, and Suriname provide safe habitats for giant armadillos, but rain forest destruction is a continuing problem. Current conservation efforts include plans to move giant armadillos to protected habitats and to breed them in captivity.

Aye–aye
Daubentonia madagascariensis

Description and biology

The unusual–looking aye–aye is covered with a coat of coarse blackish–brown hair, which overlays a denser coat of short white hair. The animal has very large, sensitive ears that stick out from its small, rounded head. It has sharp, rodent–like incisor (front) teeth and long, claw–like fingers and toes. An average aye–aye is 15 to 18 inches (38 to 46 centimeters) long from the top of its head to the end of its body. Its bushy tail measures 16 to 22 inches (41 to 56 centimeters) long. The animal weighs between 4.4 and 6.6 pounds (2 and 3 kilograms).

While an aye–aye eats bamboo shoots, sugarcane, and some small animals, most of its diet consists of fruit (especially coconuts) and wood–boring insect larvae. Using its powerful incisors, the aye–aye breaks into coconuts, then scoops out the pulp with its very long, thin middle finger. The aye–aye's large ears allow it to hear insect larvae moving beneath the bark of trees. The animal strips off the bark with its teeth, then crushes and eats the larvae with its middle finger.

The aye–aye is a nocturnal (active at night) creature. It builds a complex nest in the fork of a large tree for shelter during the day. When active, the animal spends most of its time in trees, often hanging by its hind legs. Biologists (people who study living organisms) know little about the aye–aye's social structure or mating habits. The animal's range is estimated to be 12 acres (5 hectares). A female aye–aye usually gives birth to a single infant every two to three years, and nurses the young aye–aye for up to a year.

Aye–ayes are unusual looking members of the primate family.

Habitat and current distribution

Aye–ayes are found in eastern, northern, and northwestern Madagascar, an island off the southeast coast of Africa. The animals are able to survive in a variety of forest types: deciduous (shedding plants and trees), secondary–growth, and dry scrub (stunted trees and shrubs). They have also been found in coconut groves and mangrove swamps. Although aye–aye are found over a large area of the island, their population numbers are low. Only a few thousand are believed to be alive today.

History and conservation measures

Even though its only natural predator is the fossa, a slender mammal that resembles a cat, the aye–aye was once considered one of the most endangered mammals in Madagascar. The main threat to the aye–aye is habitat destruction. Because it needs large, old trees in which to build its nest, the aye–aye cannot exist in areas that have been cleared of trees. The animal is also at risk because of superstitious fear. Many people on Madagascar believe the aye–aye brings misfortune, even death, to those it meets. For this reason, many local people kill the animal on sight and sometimes eat it. The aye–aye is also killed by local farmers, who believe the animal is a threat to crops.

Even though a number of reserves have been set up for the aye–aye in Madagascar, the protection of these areas has not been enforced. However, under a conservation program begun in 1966, nine aye–aye were released on Nosy Mangabe, a 1,300–acre (520–hectare) island off the east coast of Madagascar. These animals have received special protection, and investigations into the results of the program are ongoing.

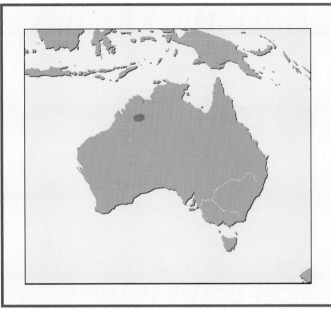

BANDICOOT, GOLDEN
Isoodon auratus

PHYLUM: Chordata
CLASS: Mammalia
ORDER: Marsupialia
FAMILY: Peramelidae
STATUS: Vulnerable, IUCN
RANGE: Australia

Bandicoot, golden
Isoodon auratus

Description and biology

The golden bandicoot belongs to the order of mammals known as marsupials, whose young continue to develop after birth in a pouch on the outside of the mother's body. The animal's coarse fur is a mixture of yellow–orange and dark brown hairs, giving it a golden appearance. It has a long, tapering snout and short, rounded ears. An average golden bandicoot measures 9 to 19 inches (23 to 48 centimeters) from the top of its head to the end of its body and weighs about 3 pounds (1.4 kilograms). Its tail is 3 to 8 inches (8 to 20 centimeters) long.

Golden bandicoot are nocturnal (active at night). During the day, they remain in their nests built on the ground, in a hollow, or in a rock pile. At night, the very quick, agile, and aggressive animals search for their diet of insects and worms. Golden bandicoot are solitary animals, so males and females come together only to mate. The female usually gives birth to a litter of four after a gestation (pregnancy) period of almost

13

Like other members of the marsupial family, female golden bandicoots contain a pouch in which their young finish developing after birth.

two weeks. The young golden bandicoot remain in their mother's pouch for up to eight weeks.

Habitat and current distribution

Golden bandicoot once ranged across one–third of Australia, mainly in grassland habitats. They are now found in a small part of the Kimberleys, a plateau region in northeastern Western Australia, and on a few islands off Australia's coast.

History and conservation measures

Scientists and conservationists (people protecting the natural world) are not quite sure why the number of golden bandicoot has decreased. They believe foxes and cats recently allowed into golden bandicoot territory have become predators of the animals. In addition, fires deliberately set by humans to manage grasslands may have destroyed the animals' natural habitat.

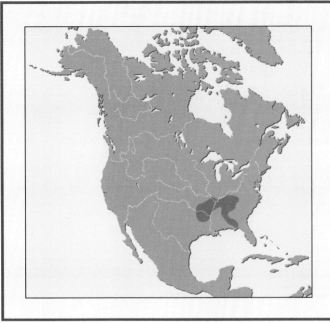

BAT, GRAY
Myotis grisescens

PHYLUM: Chordata
CLASS: Mammalia
ORDER: Chiroptera
FAMILY: Vespertilionidae
STATUS: Endangered, IUCN
Endangered, ESA
RANGE: Central and southeastern
USA

Bat, gray
Myotis grisescens

Description and biology

Contrary to its name, the gray bat is reddish–brown in color. Its forearm measures 1.6 inches (4 centimeters) long, and it weighs 0.35 ounce (10 grams). The gray bat differs from other species of the *Myotis* genus (a group with similar characteristics) in that its wing membrane (a double membrane of skin) attaches to its ankle instead of the side of its foot. The gray bat feeds at night on insects, particularly mayflies and mosquitoes. It roosts in two different types of caves throughout the year.

Female gray bats begin hibernating immediately after mating in the fall; adult males and juveniles follow several weeks later. In late March, the females emerge from hibernation, while the rest emerge about a month later. Using sperm they have stored all winter, female gray bats fertilize their eggs after hibernation, giving birth to a single infant around late May.

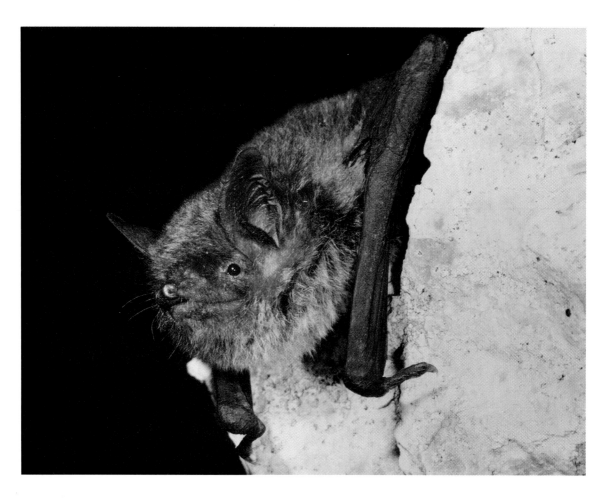

Habitat and current distribution

In summer, while gray bats are raising their young, they roost in caves that have a temperature between 57 and 77°F (14 and 25°C). In winter, during hibernation, the bats roost in caves that have a temperature between 43 and 52°F (6 and 11°C). Gray bats are found in limestone caverns in Alabama, Arkansas, Georgia, Illinois, Indiana, Kansas, Kentucky, Mississippi, Missouri, North Carolina, Oklahoma, Tennessee, and Virginia. In 1980, scientists estimated the gray bat population to be less than 1,600,000.

History and conservation measures

Before the American Civil War (1861–65), millions of gray bats inhabited the southeastern United States. Beginning with the war, bat guano (feces) was used to produce saltpeter (potassium nitrate), a component of gunpowder. When humans entered roosting caves to collect the guano, the bats were disturbed from their normal routine. This was particularly harmful during hibernation. When aroused during this period, a gray bat is forced to use its stored fat and may starve to death before spring.

In modern times, spelunking (cave exploring), tourism, and flooding caused by the construction of dams have all led to the destruction of bat habitat. Between 1960 and 1980, the gray bat population decreased almost 80 percent. Water pollution and pesticides the bats ingested by eating contaminated insects also contributed to this decline.

Since the early 1980s, many bat caves have been protected from human disturbance, and the drop in the number of gray bats seems to have stopped. Without further conservation measures, however, the bats will not reach full recovery.

BAT, TOWNSEND'S BIG-EARED
Plecotus townsendii

PHYLUM: Chordata
CLASS: Mammalia
ORDER: Chiroptera
FAMILY: Vespertilionidae
STATUS: Vulnerable, IUCN
Endangered, ESA (subspecies
ingens and *virginianus*
RANGE: Canada, Mexico, USA

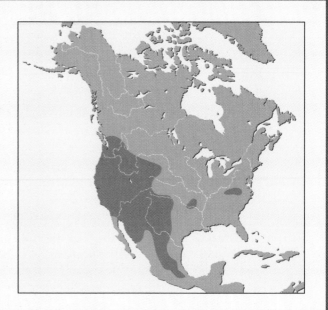

Bat, Townsend's big-eared
Plecotus townsendii

Description and biology

The Townsend's big-eared bat is named for its large ears, which are from 1 to 1.6 inches (2.5 to 4 centimeters) long. In contrast, the bat's body length is 1.8 to 2.7 inches (4.5 to 7 centimeters), its tail length is 1.4 to 2.1 inches (3.5 to 5.3 centimeters), and its forearm length is 1.4 to 2 inches (3.5 to 5 centimeters). The average Townsend's big-eared bat weighs between 0.18 and 0.46 ounce (5 and 13 grams).

Townsend's big-eared bats feed primarily on moths, which they locate through echolocation (sonar). In this process, a bat emits high-pitched sounds that echo or bounce off its prey. The bat's sensitive hearing picks up the echo. From that sound, the bat can determine the size, shape, and location of its prey.

Male and female Townsend's big-eared bats come together in late fall or early winter to mate and hibernate. The females store the sperm until early spring, when they fertilize their eggs. After a gestation (pregnancy) period of 56 to 100 days, they give birth to a single infant, which they nurse until fall.

There are five subspecies of Townsend's big–eared bat, two of which are endangered: the Ozark big–eared bat (*Plecotus townsendii ingens*) and the Virginia big–eared bat (*Plecotus townsendii virginianus*).

Habitat and current distribution

Townsend's big–eared bats are found in forest and desert areas in southwestern Canada, western United States, and Mexico. The bats inhabit caves, abandoned mines, and, sometimes, buildings. They prefer limestone caves however. Like many other species of bats, Townsend's big–eared bats hibernate in one type of cave while raising their young in another. They will often use these same sites year after year.

The gray and white Ozark big–eared bats are found only in a few caves in Arkansas, Missouri, and Oklahoma. Biologists (people who study living organisms) estimate their population to be under 700. The predominantly gray Virginia big–eared bats are found in eastern Kentucky, southwestern Virginia, and eastern West Virginia. They number approximately 11,000.

History and conservation measures

Human disturbance is the primary reason for the decline in the number of Townsend's big–eared bats. If disturbed while hibernating, the bats will often leave their roosts. Forced to rely on their stored fat for food, the bats often starve to death before winter is over.

The U.S. government has designated as critical habitats those caves known to be occupied by Townsend's big–eared bats. This act prevents federal agencies from carrying out programs that would lead to the disturbance or destruction of these caves. However, this act has not deterred vandals and curious tourists from continuing to enter protected caves.

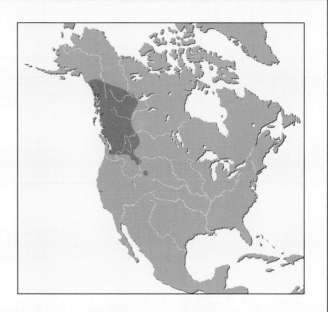

BEAR, GRIZZLY
Ursus arctos horribilis

PHYLUM: Chordata
CLASS: Mammalia
ORDER: Carnivora
FAMILY: Ursidae
STATUS: Threatened, ESA
RANGE: Canada, USA (Alaska, Idaho, Montana, Washington, Wyoming)

Bear, grizzly
Ursus arctos horribilis

Description and biology

The grizzly bear, a subspecies of the brown bear (*Ursus arctos*), is one of the largest land mammals in North America. An average male grizzly has a head and body length of 6 to 8 feet (1.8 to 2.4 meters), stands 3.5 to 4 feet (1 to 1.2 meters) at its shoulder, and may weigh up to 800 pounds (360 kilograms). The smaller female grizzly weighs between 200 and 400 pounds (90 and 180 kilograms). The grizzly bear is so–named because its thick, light brown to black fur is streaked with gray, giving it a "grizzled" look. Grizzly bears have short, rounded ears, humped shoulders, and long, curved claws.

Although grizzly bears are omnivores (they eat both plants and animals), most of their diet consists of vegetation: fruits, berries, nuts, and the bulbs and roots of plants. They also eat ants and other insects. The meat in a grizzly bear's diet comes from deer or smaller mammals such as elk or moose calves.

Salmon makes up a large part of the diet of grizzly bears that inhabit Alaska and the west coast of Canada.

Grizzly bears store large amounts of fat, which their bodies rely on during their long winter hibernation. Grizzlies build their dens in early fall, often on high, remote mountain slopes underneath the roots of large trees. Once they enter their dens in October or November, they do not emerge for five or six months (females usually emerge one month after the males in the spring).

Male and female grizzly bears usually mate in June or July. After a gestation (pregnancy) period of about six months, a female grizzly gives birth during hibernation to one to three cubs. The infant bears usually weigh 1 pound (.45 kilogram) at birth, but gain as much as 20 pounds (9 kilograms) by the time spring arrives. Female grizzlies nurse their cubs for up to one year, and the cubs remain with their mother for two to three additional years. The average life span of a grizzly bear is 15 to 20 years.

Habitat and current distribution

The grizzly bear's home range is quite large: up to 500 square miles (1,300 square kilometers) for males and 300 square miles (780 square kilometers) for females. That range may extend over a variety of forests, meadows, and grasslands in or near mountains. Grizzlies are active at lower elevations during most of the year. For hibernation, they move to higher altitudes.

In the contiguous United States (the connected 48 states), 600 to 700 grizzlies are found in Idaho, Montana, Washington, and Wyoming. Over one half of that total population inhabits the northwestern Montana Rockies. Wildlife biologists (people who study living organisms) estimate there are over 20,000 grizzly bears in western Canada and over 30,000 in Alaska (where they are called brown bears).

History and conservation measures

Grizzly bears used to range over the entire western half of North America, from Mexico up to the Arctic Circle. In 1800, the grizzly bear population in North America exceeded 50,000. By 1975, that number had been reduced to less than 1,000. Habitat destruction and hunting are the two main reasons for this drastic decline. As pioneers moved west during the nineteenth century and settled mountainous regions, grizzly bears were forced out of their natural habitat. These pioneers also shot and trapped grizzlies, believing the animals posed a threat.

As the wild areas of the American west continue to be developed (such as with the building of recreation areas), the survival of grizzly bears will continue to be jeopardized. Even though they are protected by laws, grizzlies are still shot by hunters who mistake the animals for black bears.

The U.S. government, working with state agencies and Native American tribes, has tried to manage and protect grizzly bear habitat. These efforts have been successful in areas such as the Yellowstone National Park ecosystem (plants, animals, and microorganisms with their environment), where the grizzly bear population has reached a desired level.

Bear, sun

Helarctos malayanus

Description and biology

The smallest member of the bear family, the sun bear has an average head and body length of 3.5 to 4.5 feet (1 to 1.4 meters). Its shoulder height is 26.6 inches (67.5 centimeters) and its weight is between 60 and 140 pounds (27 and 64 kilograms). The animal's short tail extends only 1 to 3 inches (3 to 7 centimeters). The fur on the sun bear's body is very short and black; the fur on its muzzle is almost white. Most animals of this species have a white to yellow–orange horseshoe–shaped marking on their chests.

The sun bear's curved and pointed claws make it an excellent climber. It spends most of its day sleeping or sunning on a platform it builds in trees 7 to 20 feet (2 to 6 meters) above the ground. It uses its strong claws to open bees' nests or to pull back the bark of trees to locate the larvae of wood–boring insects. The sun bear's diet also includes termites and other insects, fruits, birds, and small mammals. Because it is so fond of honey, the sun bear is sometimes called the honey bear.

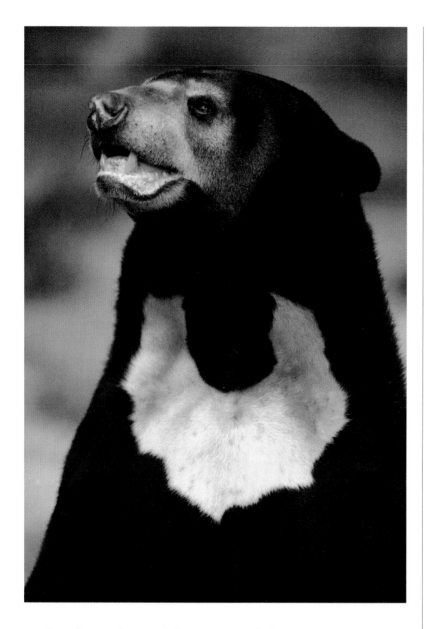

Sun bears do not hibernate, and they can mate at any time during the year. After a gestation (pregnancy) period of 95 to 240 days, a female sun bear gives birth to one or two cubs.

Habitat and current distribution

Sun bears are found scattered throughout tropical and subtropical forests in Southeast Asia.

History and conservation measures

Although biologists (people who study living organisms) are unsure of the total number of existing sun bears, they believe the population of these animals is declining. Throughout their range, the animals are killed and used for food and medicinal purposes. Korean tourists in Thailand seek out special restaurants that serve sun bear meat, believing it will enhance their health. Sun bear cubs are often captured and kept as pets.

A critical threat to sun bears is the destruction of their forest habitat to create agricultural land. A number of reserves have been set up for the animals throughout their range, but biologists do not know if these reserves provide the habitat necessary for sun bear survival.

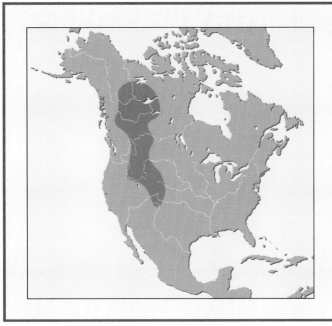

BISON, AMERICAN
Bison bison

PHYLUM: Chordata

CLASS: Mammalia

ORDER: Artiodactyla

FAMILY: Bovidae

STATUS: Lower risk: conservation dependent, IUCN Endangered, ESA (subspecies *athabascae*)

RANGE: Canada, USA

Bison, American

Bison bison

Description and biology

The American bison (commonly known as the buffalo) has a massive body, humped shoulders, and pointed horns that curve up and in. In winter, its coat is dark brown and shaggy. In the spring, this coat is shed and replaced by one that is short and light–brown. Hair on the head, neck, shoulders, and forelegs remains long and shaggy throughout the year. A beard also hangs from the chin of the animal's huge, low–slung head. An average American bison has a head and body length of 7 to 12.5 feet (2.1 to 3.8 meters) and a shoulder height of 5 to 6.5 feet (1.5 to 2 meters). It weighs between 700 and 2,200 pounds (320 and 1,000 kilograms). The animal's relatively short tail is 12 to 35 inches (31 to 89 centimeters) long and ends in a tuft of hair.

The American bison species is divided biologically into two subspecies: the plains bison (*Bison bison bison*) and the

27

Although once numbering 60,000,000 in the early nineteenth century, the American bison population now numbers less than 40,000.

wood bison (*Bison bison athabascae*). The main physical difference between the two is the color of the hair on the shoulders. On the plains bison, this hair is lighter in color than the hair on the rest of its body. The difference in hair color on the wood bison is not so pronounced.

The bison is a fast runner and good swimmer, and has a keen sense of smell. It is active during both day and night, feeding on prairie grasses and sedges (grasslike flowers). Bison usually travel in herds, although some males (bulls) tend to be solitary. Mating season lasts from June to September. The gestation (pregnancy) period of the female American bison is about 285 days. The calves, which are reddish–brown in color when born, may nurse for up to a year.

Habitat and current distribution

The total number of American bison in North America is currently about 30,000. Plains bison are found primarily in Yellowstone National Park in northwestern Wyoming, southern Montana, and eastern Idaho. This herd numbers about 2,000. Additional plains bison are located in other parks and nature reserves and on private ranches in the western United States. Wood bison exist in a number of sanctuaries in Canada, including Wood Buffalo National Park in northern Alberta and southern Northwest Territories. The number of Canadian wood buffalo is believed to be more than 5,000.

History and conservation measures

American bison once ranged from Alaska and western Canada into the United States and northern Mexico. Scientists have estimated that in the early nineteenth century more bison—60,000,000 total—existed in North America than humans. These large animals were an essential part of the culture of many Native American people, who depended on the American bison for food and clothing. As American and European settlers moved west during that century, the number of bison began to decline. The animals were hunted for their hides, meat, and tongues, which were considered a delicacy. They were shot from trains for sport. And as part of the American government's strategy to subdue Native Americans, bison were slaughtered by the millions. By the late nineteenth century, only a few hundred of each subspecies remained in the wild.

In 1902, the American government placed a herd of some 40 captive and wild plains bison under protection in Yellowstone National Park. This herd grew into the one that exists in the park today. In 1922, the Canadian government established Wood Buffalo National Park to protect the last surviving wood bison. Unfortunately, plains bison were released into the park shortly afterward, where they mated with the wood bison. The resulting offspring were a hybrid, or genetic mixture, of the two subspecies. In the late 1950s, a small herd of genetically similar wood bison were located in the park. Although scientists allowed these animals to breed only with each other, no one is certain whether any genetically pure wood bison currently exist.

Beginning in 1990, Montana Department of Livestock workers shot plains bison that wandered outside of the boundaries of Yellowstone National Park. Even though the animals are protected within the park, a state–federal agreement gives Montana officials the right to kill bison if they cross onto private land. Both Montana officials and private ranchers feared the bison would infect cattle grazing near the park with brucellosis, a disease that causes cows to abort their calves. Conservationists (people who protect the natural world) claimed that there were no cases of the disease being transmitted from a bison to a cow. Despite the lack of scientific evidence, Montana officials remained fearful. During the harsh winter of 1996–97, more than 1,000 bison that roamed outside of the park in search of food were slaughtered.

BUFFALO, WILD WATER
Bubalus bubalis

PHYLUM: Chordata
CLASS: Mammalia
ORDER: Artiodactyla
FAMILY: Bovidae
STATUS: Endangered, IUCN
RANGE: Bhutan, India, Nepal, Thailand

Buffalo, wild water

Bubalus bubalis

Description and biology

The wild water buffalo is a very large animal, averaging 7.75 to 10 feet (2.4 to 3 meters) long. It stands 5 to 6.25 feet (1.5 to 2 meters) tall at its shoulder and weighs between 1,550 and 2,650 pounds (700 and 1,200 kilograms). Long, coarse hair covers the buffalo's ash gray to black body. Both male and female water buffalo have small ears, thin faces, and widely spread horns. The horns, thick where they emerge from the animal's head, form a semicircle by curving out and back. Ending in a point, these horns may reach a length of 6 feet (2 meters).

The wild water buffalo's diet consists of grasses and other vegetation that grows along the shores of lakes and rivers. Although the animal is fast and aggressive, it can fall prey to tigers. Leopards also often prey on young water buffalo. A female water buffalo gives birth to a single infant after a gestation (pregnancy) period of 310 to 340 days. The infant is then nursed for up to nine months.

31

Grass and other vegetation make up the wild water buffalo's diet.

Habitat and current distribution

Wild water buffalo inhabit swampy or wet grassland, or river valleys with dense vegetation. The animals like to wallow in mud, which helps protect them against biting insects. To further escape insects, they will often submerge themselves in water so that only their nostrils are exposed.

Approximately 1,000 wild water buffalo survive in India and Nepal. In contrast, almost 130,000,000 domestic water buffalo, which are used to pull carts and plows, live in India and Southeast Asia. Because of interbreeding between domestic and the larger wild water buffalo, biologists (people who study living organisms) believe that less than 100 of the wild species are genetically pure.

History and conservation measures

Several factors have contributed to the disappearance of wild water buffalo: excessive hunting, the destruction of buffalo habitat to create agricultural land, and diseases transmitted by cattle and other domestic livestock. Two national parks have been set up in India to protect the remaining wild water buffalo.

CAMEL, BACTRIAN
Camelus bactrianus

PHYLUM: Chordata
CLASS: Mammalia
ORDER: Artiodactyla
FAMILY: Camelidae
STATUS: Endangered, IUCN
Endangered, ESA
RANGE: China, Mongolia

Camel, bactrian
Camelus bactrianus

Description and biology

The bactrian camel and the better–known Arabian camel (*Camelus dromedarius*) are the only two living species of true camel. Whereas the Arabian camel has only one hump, the bactrian camel has two. An average bactrian camel stands 6 to 7.5 feet (1.8 to 2.3 meters) in height and weighs between 1,000 and 1,575 pounds (455 and 715 kilograms). The coat of a wild bactrian camel is short and gray–brown in color; that of a domestic or tame version of the animal is long and dark brown.

The bactrian camel is well adapted to its desert habitat. Its special eyelids help wipe sand from the surface of the animal's eye. Its nostrils close to slits to keep out blowing sand. Its broad, thick–soled feet allow it to move steadily and quickly over shifting sand, achieving speeds up to 40 miles per hour (64 kilometers per hour). The humps of the bactrian camel

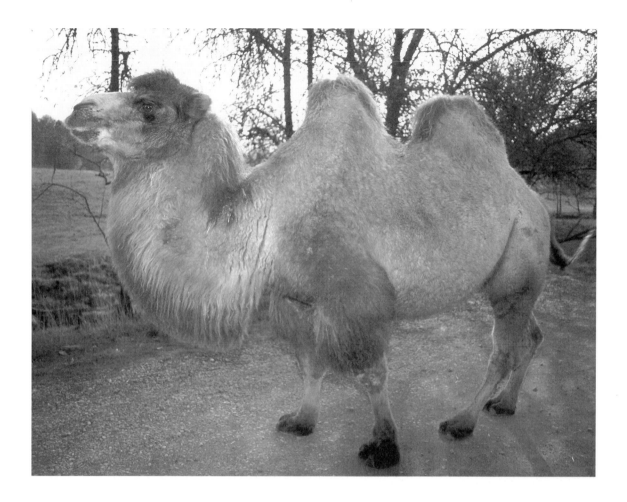

store fat like those of other camels. When full, the humps are plump and erect. If the animal has not eaten for a period of time, the humps begin to shrink and sag to one side. Bactrian camels eat mostly low–lying desert shrubs; they also may eat grasses and the leaves of trees growing near water. The camels may go without drinking water for long periods of time only if they receive enough moisture from the plants they eat.

Male bactrian camels fight for the opportunity to mate with female bactrian camels. The competitions between males are quite fierce and some end in death. A dominant male will gather a group of 10 to 20 females with which to mate. After a gestation (pregnancy) period of almost 13 months, a female bactrian camel gives birth to a single infant, usually in March or April. The infant camel, weighing about 80 pounds (36 kilograms) at birth, nurses for at least its first year.

Bactrian camels are well adapted to their desert environment. They are able to go for long periods without water by eating plants containing moisture.

Habitat and current distribution

Wild bactrian camels inhabit desert and steppe (semiarid, grass–covered plain) areas in lowland and mountain regions. In Mongolia, they are found in and around the Great Gobi National Park, a protected area of the Gobi Desert located in southwestern Mongolia. Biologists (people who study living organisms) estimate that 500 to 600 camels live in this area. In China, an estimated 500 wild bactrian camels are found in the western provinces of Xinjiang (Sinkiang) and Gansu (Kansu).

History and conservation measures

Humans in China and Mongolia probably began to use bactrian camels as pack animals to carry supplies as far back as 2500 B.C. Up until the beginning of the twentieth century, the range of wild bactrian camels extended from Asia Minor to northern China. As human populations grew in this large area, the camels were confined to a smaller and smaller range.

Habitat loss continues to be a major threat to the bactrian camel. Both Chinese and Mongolian governments have declared the camel a protected species. Three reserves have been established to safeguard the animals: the Great Gobi National Park in Mongolia, the Annaba Nature Reserve in Gansu, and the Altun Mountain Nature Reserve in Xinjiang. However, wolves continually prey on bactrian camels in the Gobi Park, and those camels that stray outside of the park are often killed for food by humans. Interbreeding with domestic camels has further reduced the population of genetically pure wild bactrian camels. These factors plus the lack of well–developed conservation plans—especially in China—put the survival of the wild bactrian camel at risk.

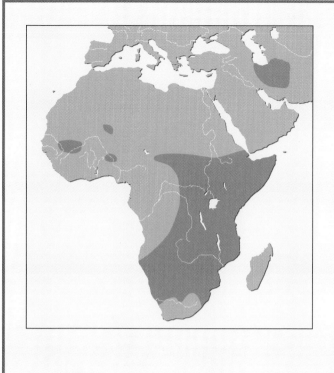

CHEETAH
Acinonyx jubatus

PHYLUM: Chordata
CLASS: Mammalia
ORDER: Carnivora
FAMILY: Felidae
STATUS: Vulnerable, IUCN Endangered, ESA
RANGE: Afghanistan, Algeria, Angola, Benin, Botswana, Burkina Faso, Cameroon, Central African Republic, Chad, Congo, Egypt, Ethiopia, India, Iran, Jordan, Kenya, Libya, Malawi, Mali, Mauritania, Morocco, Mozambique, Namibia, Niger, Nigeria, Pakistan, Saudi Arabia, Senegal, Somalia, South Africa, Sudan, Swaziland, Tanzania, Togo, Uganda, Western Sahara, Zambia, Zimbabwe

Cheetah

Acinonyx jubatus

Description and biology

"Cheetah" comes from the Hindu word *chita*, meaning "spotted one." Round black spots cover the cheetah's tawny fur and a black streak runs down each cheek. An average cheetah measures 4.5 to 5 feet (1.4 to 1.5 meters) long and stands between 27 and 34 inches (69 and 86 centimeters) high at its shoulder. Its tail extends 24 to 32 inches (61 to 81 centimeters). It weighs between 80 and 145 pounds (36 and 66 kilograms).

Cheetahs are the world's fastest land animal. They are capable of bursts of speed up to 70 miles per hour (110 kilometers per hour), but they usually cannot keep up this top speed for more than 1500 feet (455 meters).

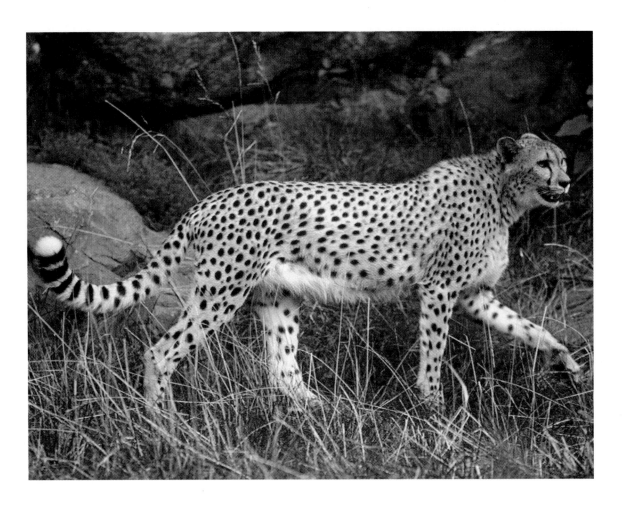

A cheetah prowling for prey, which may include gazelles, wildebeest, antelope, warthogs, hares, and ground birds.

Unlike other cats, a cheetah cannot retract its claws. This physical feature allows the animal to dig into the ground as it runs, giving it speed. Whereas leopards and tigers ambush their prey, cheetahs chase their prey down. Because they exert themselves so much when catching prey, cheetahs often have to rest for up to half an hour before they can eat. Typical cheetah prey includes gazelles, wildebeest, antelope, warthogs, hares, and ground birds.

Male cheetahs often live with their male littermates (brothers) in groups called coalitions. Much more solitary, female cheetahs join their male counterparts only to mate. After a gestation (pregnancy) period of 90 to 95 days, a female cheetah gives birth to a litter of one to eight cubs, which she nurses for three months. Because she must provide her cubs with fresh kill almost every day, a female cheetah's hunting territory may cover as much as 310 square miles (800 square kilometers). She will frequently bring small, live prey to her cubs to help them develop hunting skills.

Habitat and current distribution

Cheetahs prefer to inhabit savannas and other arid (dry), open grasslands. The animals are now restricted to Africa south of the Sahara Desert. The largest number of cheetahs are found in Namibia and East Africa. Wildlife biologists (people who study living organisms) estimate that the total population ranges from 5,000 to 12,000. A small group of cheetahs numbering about 200 was found recently in northern Iran.

History and conservation measures

Cheetahs once ranged over Africa, Arabia, the Middle East, and northern India. Since they can be tamed, cheetahs have been kept for centuries by kings and noblemen as pets and hunting animals. In the mid–1950s, the cheetah population was estimated to be 28,000. Within twenty years, however, that number was cut in half.

Hunting and habitat destruction are the main causes for this drastic decline. Although cheetahs are legally protected in most countries, poachers still hunt them for their fur, which remains popular in Asia and Europe. Farmers also kill cheetahs, believing the animals might harm their livestock. As grassland is converted into pasture and agricultural land, cheetahs are confined to smaller and smaller areas, limiting their hunting ability.

Reserves have been set up in Africa, but in these protected areas cheetahs face fierce competition from predators such as lions and hyenas. Some African countries like Namibia have tried to introduce cheetahs into areas where they would face few animal or human predators.

CHIMPANZEE
Pan troglodytes

PHYLUM: Chordata
CLASS: Mammalia
ORDER: Primates
FAMILY: Pongidae
STATUS: Endangered, IUCN
Endangered, ESA
RANGE: Burundi, Cameroon,
Central African Republic, Congo,
Congo Republic, Côte d'Ivoire,
Equatorial Guinea, Gabon,
Gambia, Ghana, Guinea,
Guinea–Bissau, Liberia, Mali,
Nigeria, Rwanda, Senegal, Sierra
Leone, Sudan, Tanzania, Uganda

Chimpanzee

Pan troglodytes

Description and biology

Chimpanzees, gorillas, and orangutans are all considered great apes. Of the three, chimpanzees are the most closely related to humans. Chimpanzees and humans share 98 percent of the same genetic makeup. In addition, the two groups share many social and psychological traits. Researchers have documented chimpanzees making and using tools, expressing complex emotions, forming bonds and friendships, and communicating using sign language.

An average chimpanzee stands 5 feet (1.5 meters) tall and weighs about 150 pounds (68 kilograms). Since its arms are longer than its legs, a chimpanzee walks on the ground using the soles of its feet and the knuckles of its hands. Most of its body is covered with long, black hair. A chimpanzee's hairless face can range in color from almost white to almost black.

The hair around a chimpanzee's face grays with age, and older chimpanzees often become bald.

Highly social mammals, chimpanzees live in communities made up of 30 to 60 members. During the day, the animals often travel on the ground. At night, they stay in nests they build in treetops. A chimpanzee's diet consists mainly of fruit, but they also eat insects, leaves, flowers, bark, seeds, tree resin, eggs, and meat. At times, chimpanzees band together to hunt animals such as antelopes and monkeys.

Mating between male and female chimpanzees takes place anytime during the year. Unlike many other animal species, female chimpanzees do not have to mate with the dominant male in their group. Instead, females often mate with males of their choosing. After a gestation (pregnancy) period of 230 to 240 days, a female chimpanzee gives birth to a single infant. During the course of her life, an average female chimpanzee will give birth to less than five infants. Bonds between mothers and infants are very strong, and some last a lifetime.

Habitat and current distribution

A few centuries ago, several million chimpanzees existed in the equatorial regions of Africa. They inhabited a range of ecosystems, from dense forests to open savannas. Now, less than 300,000 chimpanzees exist in the wild. Only 11 present–day African nations have chimpanzee populations above 1,000.

About 5,000 chimpanzees exist in captivity worldwide. Over one–half of these are used as subjects in medical research. The rest are zoo exhibits, entertainment props, and private pets.

History and conservation measures

Habitat destruction, disease, and expanding human populations have led to the decline in the number of chimpanzees. Mining has destroyed the chimpanzee habitat in the diamond districts of Sierra Leone and the iron districts of Liberia. The cutting of forests for timber has destroyed the animals' habitat in Uganda. And the conversion of forests into agricultural land has threatened chimpanzees in Rwanda and Burundi.

Certain laws prohibit the hunting and sale of chimpanzees, but these laws are not enforced. Many chimpanzees are caught and traded illegally. For each chimpanzee shipped overseas, ten die during transport due to mistreatment and malnutrition.

Two sanctuaries exist in Gambia and Zambia for orphaned chimpanzees and those seized from illegal traders. Most African nations have passed laws and have set aside areas to protect chimpanzees. However, as human populations in Africa continue to grow, many of these reserves may be used to fill human needs.

CHINCHILLA, SHORT–TAILED
Chinchilla brevicaudata

PHYLUM: Chordata
CLASS: Mammalia
ORDER: Rodentia
FAMILY: Chinchillidae
STATUS: Critically endangered,
IUCN
Endangered, ESA
RANGE: Argentina, Bolivia, Chile,
Peru

Chinchilla, short–tailed

Chinchilla brevicaudata

Description and biology

The short–tailed chinchilla is a nocturnal (active at night) rodent with soft fur, large ears, and a bushy tail. It is one of two species of chinchilla—the other is the long–tailed chinchilla (*Chinchilla langiera*). An average chinchilla has a head and body length between 9 and 15 inches (23 and 38 centimeters) and a tail length between 3 and 6 inches (7.5 and 15 centimeters). Female chinchillas weigh up to 28 ounces (794 grams), while the smaller males weigh up to 18 ounces (510 grams). A chinchilla's silky fur is mostly gray in color. The animal's hind legs are much larger than its front legs, making it an agile jumper.

A chinchilla's diet includes leaves, seeds, fruits, and other vegetation. While eating, it often stands erect and holds the

43

The demand for the short–tailed chinchillas' fur has lead to the animals becoming endangered.

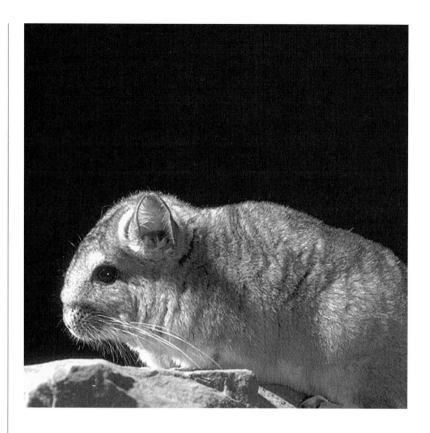

food with its forepaws. A female chinchilla may give birth to up to six infants at a time.

Habitat and current distribution

Short–tailed chinchillas prefer to live in the mountainous regions of Argentina, Bolivia, Chile, and Peru at elevations over 6,560 feet (2,000 meters). They live among crevices and rocks in barren areas covered with dense shrubs and grasses. The number of short–tailed chinchillas in the wild is unknown, but centuries of hunting has severely reduced their population.

History and conservation measures

Humans have prized chinchilla fur since the days of the Inca, native Quechuan people of Peru who established an empire in South America in the fifteenth century. Between 1895 and 1900, 1,680,000 chinchilla skins were exported from the country of Chile alone. Coats made from the animal's soft fur have sold for over $100,000. Since the 1920s, millions of chinchillas have been raised on farms for use in the fur industry.

Before laws were passed protecting wild chinchillas, hunters almost made the animals extinct. Reserves have been established to provide wild short–tailed chinchillas with a protected habitat, but illegal hunting still threatens their survival.

DEER, MUSK
Moschus spp. (all species)

PHYLUM: Chordata
CLASS: Mammalia
ORDER: Artiodactyla
FAMILY: Moschidae
STATUS: Vulnerable, IUCN
(*Moschus moschiferus*)
Endangered, ESA (all species)
RANGE: Afghanistan, Bhutan,
China, India, Mongolia, Myanmar,
Nepal, North Korea, Pakistan,
Russia, South Korea, Vietnam

Deer, musk

Moschus spp. (all species)

Description and biology

Musk deer are so–named because the males of the species have a gland, called the pod, that develops in the skin of their abdomen. This gland produces a waxy substance called musk, which may be used by males to attract females. An average musk deer has a head and body length of 28 to 39 inches (71 to 99 centimeters), stands 20 to 24 inches (51 to 91 centimeters) at its shoulder, and weighs between 15 and 40 pounds (7 and 18 kilograms). The musk deer's hair is long and coarse. It varies in color from dark to golden brown, depending on the species.

The hind legs of a musk deer are almost one–third larger than its front legs. This helps to make the animal a quick and agile jumper. Unlike most other deer, musk deer have no antlers. The upper canine teeth of male musk deer grow into narrow, pointed tusks that curve down and backward from the animal's mouth. Males use these 2.5– to 3–inch (6.3– to

7.6–centimeter) teeth when fighting each other over the right to mate with females.

Mating takes place in November and December. A male musk deer pursues a female until she is too exhausted to run anymore. After a gestation (pregnancy) period of 150 to 198 days, a female musk deer gives birth to one or two infants, which are born with spotted coats.

Musk deer feed on leaves, flowers, twigs, mosses, grasses, and lichen (an organism formed by algae and fungus growing together) during morning and evening hours. Predators of musk deer include the lynx, wolf, fox, and yellow–throated marten (mammal related to the weasel and the mink).

Musk deers are often killed by hunters in order to obtain the animals' musk which is used in perfumes and medicines.

Habitat and current distribution

Musk deer inhabit wet forests in the Himalayas, eastern Asia, and Siberia. During summer, the animals can be found in mountain forests ranging over 8,500 feet (2,600 meters) in elevation. They prefer dense vegetation and brush so they can easily find shelter during the day.

Wildlife biologists (people who study living organisms) are unsure of the total number of all species of musk deer in existence. They believe the population to be between 30,000 and 100,000. Of the five main species of musk deer, the Siberian musk deer (*Moschus moschiferus*) is the most threatened.

History and conservation measures

Humans have hunted musk deer not for their meat or hide, but solely for their musk, which is used in perfumes and medicines. Hunting and habitat destruction endanger the present–day survival of all musk deer species.

Musk deer do not have to be killed in order to extract their musk. A program to raise the animals and extract their musk without causing injury began in China in the late 1950s. After the program proved successful, similar programs were implemented in India, Nepal, and Russia.

DEER, SWAMP
Cervus duvauceli

PHYLUM: Chordata
CLASS: Mammalia
ORDER: Artiodactyla
FAMILY: Cervidae
STATUS: Vulnerable, IUCN
Endangered, ESA
RANGE: India, Nepal

Deer, swamp

Cervus duvauceli

Description and biology

The swamp deer is a large member of the deer family. The animal has an average head and body length of 4 to 6 feet (1.2 to 1.8 meters), measures about 4 feet (1.2 meters) in height at its shoulder, and weighs between 375 and 620 pounds (170 and 280 kilograms). In winter, the swamp deer's coat is brown on the top part of its body and paler on its underside. In summer, the entire coat lightens in color. Male swamp deer are often darker overall than females. Swamp deer feed on grasses and aquatic plants, and their main predators are tigers and leopards.

In central India, swamp deer are known as barasingha, which means six–pointer. However, their 36– to 40–inch (91– to 102–centimeter) antlers can have 10 or more points. Antlers are solid, bony outgrowths of a deer's skull. The stem of an

Although often called barasingah (six-pointer) in India, swamp deers can have ten or more points on their antlers.

antler is called the beam, while the branches are called the tines. Most male deer grow and shed antlers annually.

Like male deer of other species, male swamp deer use their antlers when competing with each other over the right to mate with females. A dominant male may mate with as many as 30 females during mating season, which lasts from September to April. After a gestation (pregnancy) period of 225 to 250 days, a female swamp deer gives birth to a single infant.

Habitat and current distribution

Swamp deer are found scattered throughout Nepal and northern, central, and far eastern India. Almost 5,000 swamp deer inhabit the marshy grasslands and floodplains of the northern regions. In the remaining habitat areas, about 600 swamp deer live in drier woodlands and fields.

History and conservation measures

Scientists estimate that thousands of swamp deer lived along the major rivers of India during the nineteenth century. Now, most swamp deer live in protected reserves such as the Sukla Phanta Preserve in Nepal, the Dudhwa National Park in northern India, and the Kanha National Park in central India.

Habitat destruction has been the leading cause for the decline in the population of swamp deer. Illegal hunting and competition from other deer species for food and habitat also continue to threaten its existence.

DOG, AFRICAN WILD
Lycaon pictus

PHYLUM: Chordata
CLASS: Mammalia
ORDER: Carnivora
FAMILY: Canidae
STATUS: Endangered, IUCN
Endangered, ESA
RANGE: Algeria, Angola, Benin, Botswana, Burkina Faso, Burundi, Cameroon, Central African Republic, Chad, Congo, Congo Republic, Côte d'Ivoire, Eritrea, Ethiopia, Gabon, Gambia, Ghana, Guinea, Kenya, Malawi, Mali, Mozambique, Namibia, Niger, Nigeria, Rwanda, Senegal, Sierra Leone, Somalia, South Africa, Sudan, Swaziland, Tanzania, Togo, Uganda, Zambia, Zimbabwe

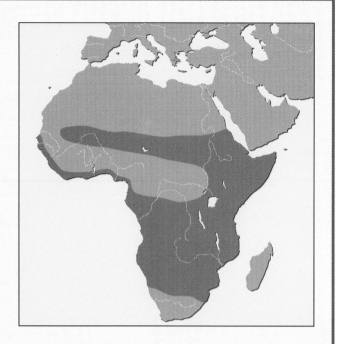

Dog, African wild
Lycaon pictus

Description and biology

The African wild dog, also called the African painted wolf, has a streaked, multicolored coat. The tan, black, and white pattern varies between individual dogs, but each animal's head is usually dark. An African wild dog has large rounded ears, which it uses to signal other dogs and to control body temperature by radiating (giving off) heat. Its 12– to 16–inch (30– to 41–centimeter) tail ends in a plume that is white–tipped. The dog's legs are long and thin. An average African wild dog has a head and body length of 30 to 44 inches (76 to 112 centimeters) and a shoulder height of 24 to 31 inches (61 to 79 centimeters). It weighs between 37 and 79 pounds (17 and 36 kilograms).

African wild dogs have a tightly knit social structure. They form packs of 2 to 45 members that hunt cooperatively. Prey includes impalas, antelopes, gazelles, zebras, wildebeest, and warthogs. The dogs are swift runners and can reach speeds up to 40 miles (64 kilometers) per hour. Their hunting range varies widely from 600 to 1,500 square miles (1,555 to 3,885 square kilometers).

In a pack, all males are related to each other and all females are related to each other, but males and females are not related. Male and female groups often travel from packs to join new ones. In most cases, mating takes place between the dominant male and dominant female in a pack. After a gestation (pregnancy) period of 69 to 72 days, a female African wild dog gives birth to up to 16 pups. About half of these pups do not survive infancy. All members of the pack

An African wild dog and her pups in their den. A female wild dog can give birth to up to 16 pups, but probably only half of these will survive infancy.

care for the pups, which are allowed to eat first after the pack makes a kill.

Habitat and current distribution

African wild dogs are found throughout Africa south of the Sahara Desert. The animals prefer to inhabit grasslands, savannas, or open woodlands. Biologists (people who study living organisms) estimate that about 5,000 African wild dogs currently exist in the world.

History and conservation measures

African wild dogs were once common throughout the African continent. At the beginning of the twentieth century, packs of 100 or more dogs roamed the Serengeti Plain in northern Tanzania. Today, the total number of African wild dogs on the Serengeti is less than 60.

As the human population in Africa has grown, wild dog habitat has decreased. The animals have also suffered because of the widespread—but unfounded—belief they are pests. In many areas in Africa, people have shot, poisoned, and trapped them. The greatest threat to African wild dogs, however, is increased contact with domestic dogs. Canine diseases such as distemper and rabies run rampant when introduced into an African wild dog pack.

The breeding of African wild dogs in zoos has been moderately successful.

DOLPHIN, CHINESE RIVER

Lipotes vexillifer

PHYLUM: Chordata
CLASS: Mammalia
ORDER: Cetacea
FAMILY: Platanistidae
STATUS: Critically endangered, IUCN
Endangered, ESA
RANGE: China

Dolphin, Chinese river
Lipotes vexillifer

Description and biology

The Chinese river dolphin, also known as baiji, is one of the most rare and endangered cetaceans (pronounced si–TAY–shuns; the order of aquatic mammals that includes whales, dolphins, and porpoises). It has an average overall length of 6.75 to 8.25 feet (2 to 2.5 meters) and weighs between 220 and 500 pounds (100 and 230 kilograms). Its body color is blue–gray on top and almost white underneath.

Chinese river dolphins have very poor eyesight, which is an evolutionary result of the muddy conditions of the water in which they live. Since the dolphins could not use their vision, they lost it over the course of time. The species adapted to this loss by developing the ability to use echolocation (sonar). In this process, the dolphin emits a sound wave that bounces off objects and is echoed or reflected back to the dolphin. Like bats, Chinese river dolphins use echolocation to navigate and to find prey.

The dolphins usually travel in pairs or in groups of up to 10. The mating season for Chinese river dolphins occurs between March and May and again between August and October. A female dolphin gives birth to a single calf after a gestation (pregnancy) period of 10 to 11 months. During its first year, the young dolphin may swim behind its mother or the mother may carry it with her flipper.

Habitat and current distribution

Chinese river dolphins are found only in the Changjiang (Yangtze River) in China. They inhabit the middle and lower reaches of the main river and often congregate where fish gather, such as around sandbanks or where tributaries and lakes connect to the main river. Scientists estimate that the entire population of Chinese river dolphins is less than 200.

History and conservation measures

Many factors have led to the current critically endangered status of the Chinese river dolphin. Fishermen on the Changjiang often try to snag bottom–feeding fish by dragging hooks along the river's bottom. This illegal fishing method accounts for about one–half of the known Chinese river dolphin deaths. Other dolphins are killed by boat propellers, especially in the lower region of the river where boat traffic is dense. A number of dolphins are killed when construction crews use explosives to build dams along the river. When built, dams and other barriers on the Changjiang destroy the dolphins' habitat and food sources, leading to further deaths.

Since the late 1970s, the Chinese government has tried to protect the Chinese river dolphin. Programs are being developed to establish reserve areas on the river where fishing and fast boat traffic would be prohibited. Unless drastic conservation measures are taken, however, the Chinese river dolphin will become extinct in the wild.

ELEPHANT, AFRICAN
Loxodonta africana

PHYLUM: Chordata
CLASS: Mammalia
ORDER: Proboscidea
FAMILY: Elephantidae
STATUS: Endangered, IUCN Threatened, ESA
RANGE: Angola, Benin, Botswana, Burkina Faso, Cameroon, Central African Republic, Chad, Congo, Congo Republic, Côte d'Ivoire, Equatorial Guinea, Ethiopia, Gabon, Ghana, Guinea, Kenya, Liberia, Malawi, Mali, Mauritania, Mozambique, Namibia, Niger, Nigeria, Rwanda, Senegal, Sierra Leone, Somalia, South Africa, Sudan, Tanzania, Togo, Uganda, Zambia, Zimbabwe

Elephant, African
Loxodonta africana

Description and biology

The African elephant is the world's largest living land mammal. An average adult male stands 10 feet (3 meters) tall at its shoulder and weighs between 11,000 and 13,000 pounds (5,000 and 5,900 kilograms). Females are a little shorter in height and weigh about 8,000 pounds (3,600 kilograms). The animal's thick and loose skin is dark, muddy gray in color. Its large ears, up to 42 inches (107 centimeters) in diameter, hold many prominent veins. To cool its blood during the heat of the day, the African elephant flaps its ears vigorously. Its long, white tusks are actually elongated incisor teeth. It has only four other teeth, all molars, that it uses to grind down food. These teeth are replaced up to six times as they wear away periodically during an average elephant's seventy–year life span.

Besides its tusks, a unique feature of the elephant is its trunk, which is an extension of its nose and upper lip. The animal uses its trunk for drinking, bathing, smelling, breathing, feeling, greeting, communicating, and grasping. The African elephant has two fingerlike tips at the end of its trunk that are sensitive enough to pick up very small objects.

African elephants are herbivores (plant–eaters), consuming tree bark, fruits, grasses, and leaves of trees and shrubs. They require approximately 300 to 400 pounds (135 to 180 kilograms) of food and 50 gallons (190 liters) of water a day. The animals never stray far from a source of water, which they use for drinking, bathing, and cooling. After bathing each day, the elephants coat themselves in dust and dirt for protection against insects.

The elephants are social animals that form strong family ties. Family units or herds are made up females (called cows) and their young (calves). The entire herd is led by an older cow called the matriarch, to which all other members of the herd are related. When a member of the herd dies, other members "grieve" over the loss, covering the dead elephant with leaves and twigs and staying by the grave for hours.

Older male elephants (bulls) live by themselves or with other males in small groups called bachelor herds. They associate with females only to breed. After a gestation (pregnancy) period of almost two years, a female elephant gives birth to a single calf, which weighs between 200 and 300 pounds (90 and 136 kilograms). Other females are often present during the birth and help keep predators away. The calf nurses for at least two years and remains dependent on the mother for four to five years.

Habitat and current distribution

African elephants are found in most areas of Africa south of the Sahara Desert. Biologists (people who study living organisms) estimate that 500,000 of these animals currently exist in the wild, primarily in southern Africa. Those elephants living in central or western Africa inhabit forest areas, while the elephants in the eastern and southern regions of the continent live in savanna and bush habitats.

History and conservation measures

African elephants have been hunted for centuries for their tusks, which are composed of ivory. This substance has been used to make items ranging from jewelry to piano keys. The animals once ranged in northern Africa up to the Mediterranean coast, but they became extinct there during the European Middle Ages (450–1450).

As the human population in Africa continues to grow, the elephant's habitat continues to shrink. In the late 1970s, African elephants numbered approximately 1,500,000. Less the 20 years later, that number has been decreased by two–thirds.

The greatest threat to the future of African elephants continues to be poaching, or illegal killing. Steps have been taken to protect the animals from poachers. Several African countries have established elephant conservation programs. National parks and reserve areas have been set aside to safeguard the animals and allow tourists to see them in their natural habitat.

In 1989, the Convention on International Trade in Endangered Species of Wild Fauna and Flora (CITES; an international treaty to protect wildlife) adopted a ban on the sale of elephant ivory. The international market for ivory immediately decreased. In June 1997, that ban was lifted when a majority of CITES member nations voted to allow the African countries of Botswana, Namibia, and Zimbabwe to sell 59 tons of stockpiled elephant tusks to Japan. The sale, estimated to bring in $30,000,000, was allowed as a reward for the conservation efforts of the three countries. Opponents of the sale believed it would simply encourage renewed African elephant slaughters by poachers.

ELEPHANT, ASIAN
Elephas maximus

PHYLUM: Chordata
CLASS: Mammalia
ORDER: Proboscidea
FAMILY: Elephantidae
STATUS: Endangered, IUCN
Endangered, ESA
RANGE: Bangladesh, Bhutan,
Brunei, Cambodia, China, India,
Indonesia, Laos, Malaysia,
Myanmar, Nepal, Sri Lanka,
Thailand, Vietnam

Elephant, Asian
Elephas maximus

Description and biology

The Asian elephant, also known as the Indian elephant, is smaller than its relative, the African elephant. An average male Asian elephant weighs up to 11,500 pounds (5,220 kilograms) and stands 8.5 feet (2.6 meters) tall at its shoulder. Females of the species are slightly shorter in height and weigh up to 6,000 pounds (2,270 kilograms). The elephant has an arched back and a flat forehead. Its ears are smaller and its trunk shorter and smoother than those of the African elephant.

The Asian elephant's trunk, which is an extension of its nose and upper lip, has one fingerlike tip at the end that is used to grasp food and other items. Elephants also use their trunks for drinking, bathing, smelling, breathing, feeling, greeting, and communicating. All of the animals can create a variety of sounds with their trunks, from rumbling noises to the well–known trumpeting sound.

Unlike African elephants, only some male Asian elephants (and no females) have tusks, which are enlarged incisor teeth. Like its relative, the Asian elephant has four molar teeth, which are replaced up to six times during its lifetime. When the final set of teeth are worn out, the elephant can no longer chew its food, and it dies of starvation.

Asian elephants feed on more than 100 species of plants, including grasses, leaves, twigs, roots, and bark. The animals spend 17 to 18 hours foraging for the 330 pounds (150 kilograms) of food they require each day. They need large areas of forest habitat to supply this food, but they never travel far from a source of water, which they use daily for drinking and bathing.

Elephants have a close and complex social structure. Related females (mothers, daughters, sisters) and their young form herds headed by an older related female, called the matriarch. Older males live singly or together in a small group known as a bachelor herd. The relationships elephants form with each other last a lifetime, which is up to 70 years. When a member of a herd dies, the other members cover the dead body with leaves and twigs, then remain at the site for hours.

Males and females associate with each other only for mating and sometimes for feeding. After a gestation (pregnancy) period of 18 to 22 months, a female Asian elephant gives birth to a single calf. The calf nurses and remains dependent on its mother for three to four years.

Habitat and current distribution

Asian elephants once ranged from Iraq to southern China. They now occupy the forests and jungles of India, Sri Lanka, China, Indonesia, and southeast Asia. Biologists (people who study living organisms) estimate that about 55,000 Asian elephants remain in the wild, occupying a habitat of only about 190,000 square miles (492,000 square kilometers). The largest population is found in India.

History and conservation measures

Humans have domesticated Asian elephants for centuries, using them to carry people and goods. The elephants have been used extensively in the timber industry, carrying items such as logs with their trunks.

Because many Asian elephants do not have tusks, they have not been hunted to supply the ivory trade as much as African elephants have (tusks are composed of ivory, a substance that has been used to make items ranging from jewelry to piano keys). Nevertheless, the Asian elephant faces greater threats to its existence than its African relative.

Deforestation, the loss of forests as they are cut down to produce timber or to make land available for agriculture, has had a devastating impact on Asian elephants. The animals need large forest areas to supply their daily food needs. Growing human populations in the region (in India alone, the human population has more than tripled in the twentieth century) have converted vast areas of forested land into farmland. As a result, much of the elephant's habitat has been reduced, and they are forced to live in pockets of forest surrounded by cultivated land. Seeking food, they often eat crops planted on farms that were once their feeding grounds. This brings them into greater conflict with humans.

Asian elephants are still used in the Asian timber industry. Unless protected areas are set for the animals and human populations stabilize in the region, the continued survival of Asian elephants is in jeopardy.

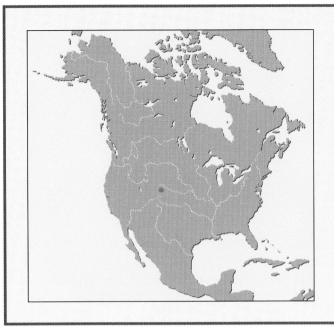

FERRET, BLACK–FOOTED
Mustela nigripes

PHYLUM: Chordata
CLASS: Mammalia
ORDER: Carnivora
FAMILY: Mustelidae
STATUS: Extinct in the wild, IUCN
Endangered, ESA
RANGE: USA (reintroduced in Wyoming)

Ferret, black–footed

Mustela nigripes

Description and biology

The black–footed ferret is a member of the weasel family (other members include weasels, martens, fishers, otters, minks, wolverines, and skunks). Similar in size to a mink, the back–footed ferret has a long, slender body covered in short, pale yellow fur. On its throat and belly, the fur is nearly white. The animal has a brownish head, a brownish–black mask across its eyes, black feet and legs, and a black tip on its tail. An average black–footed ferret has a body length of 18 to 22 inches (46 to 59 centimeters) and a tail length of 4.5 to 5.5 inches (11.5 to 14 centimeters). It weighs 18 to 36 ounces (510 to 1,021 grams).

Black–footed ferrets prey on prairie dogs and live in prairie dog burrows. They hunt at night and are rarely active above ground during the day. Ferrets also eat mice, voles, ground squirrels, gophers, birds, and insects. They are preyed upon by great–horned owls, golden eagles, coyotes, and badgers.

Ferrets are solitary animals. They move around a territorial range of about 100 acres (40 hectares), which they mark with musk from scent glands. Males often have a larger range than females. The two sexes only come together to mate in March and April. After a gestation (pregnancy) period of 41 to 45 days, a female black–footed ferret gives birth to three to five infants, called kits. The kits do not come out of the burrow until they are six weeks old. Then the mother separates the kits into different burrows, where they learn to take care of themselves. By early fall, they are on their own. Most kits do not survive their first year, and most adult ferrets do not live more than a few years.

Habitat and current distribution

Black–footed ferrets once ranged throughout the Great Plains—from Texas to southern Saskatchewan, Canada, and from the Rocky Mountains to the Dakotas, Nebraska, and Kansas. Considered one of the most endangered mammals in the United States, the black–footed ferret did not exist in the wild between 1987 and 1991.

History and conservation measures

When American pioneers moved west across the plains in the nineteenth and early twentieth centuries, they destroyed prairie dog habitat in order to create land for livestock and agriculture. The use of poison, hunting, and habitat destruction reduced the prairie dog population by 90 percent. As prairie dogs and their habitat disappeared, so did the food sources and habitat for black–footed ferrets. A severe plague of canine distemper (viral disease) in the 1950s further reduced the small number of remaining black–footed ferrets.

Because no black–footed ferrets were found in the wild between 1972 and 1981, the animal was thought to be extinct. However, in 1981, a small population of ferrets was discovered near Meeteetse, Wyoming. The population increased over the next few years, but an outbreak of canine distemper in 1985 severely threatened the survival of the species.

In 1987, the U.S. Fish and Wildlife Service (USFWS) placed the last 18 known wild black–footed ferrets in a captive breeding facility. The goal of this program is to maintain a breeding population of black–footed ferrets in captivity and to return their offspring to the wild. In 1991, 49 captive–bred, young ferrets were released into the Shirley Basin in Wyoming. Several of these animals survived the winter and have bred successfully.

Since then, almost 200 captive–bred ferrets have been released in Wyoming. The USFWS plans to release more black–footed ferrets at sites in Montana and South Dakota. Future sites may be established in Arizona, Colorado, and Utah.

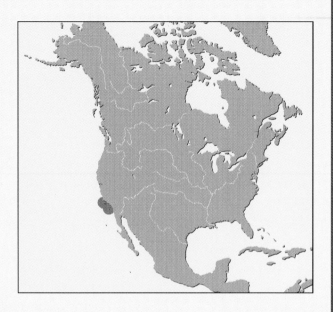

Fox, island gray

Urocyon littoralis

Description and biology

While the island gray fox is mostly gray, its belly and throat are white, and the sides of its neck and the underside of its tail are rust. Black markings often accent its face and limbs. An average island gray fox has a head and body length of 20 inches (50 centimeters) and stands roughly 5 inches (13 centimeters) tall at its shoulder. Its tail can extend in length from 4.5 to 11.5 inches (11.4 to 29.2 centimeters). It weighs between 3 and 6 pounds (1.3 and 2.7 kilograms).

The island gray fox hunts for food primarily in the early morning and late evening. Insects and fruits constitute the main portion of its diet, with small mammals, birds, reptiles, and eggs making up the remainder.

Male and female foxes come together to mate between December and March. A female island gray fox usually gives birth to a litter of one to eight pups after a gestation (pregnancy) period of 50 to 60 days. The mother nurses her pups for six weeks while the father hunts for food in a range of about 3 square miles (7.7 square kilometers).

Habitat and current distribution

The island gray fox is found only on the six largest Santa Barbara Islands (also known as the Channel Islands) that extend along the southern coast of California. It lives in a variety of habitats, including grassland, coastal scrub, sand dune, and forest areas.

History and conservation measures

At present, the island gray fox population seems stable. However, the species' long–term safety is uncertain. Destruction of its limited habitat is the main threat to the animal's continued existence. Other threats include competition for food from feral (once domesticated, now wild) cats and possible diseases from domestic dogs.

The remoteness of the Santa Barbara Islands makes protection of the island gray fox difficult. The U.S. Navy is attempting to eliminate feral cats on the islands of San Clemente and San Nicolas. Also, the Los Angeles Zoo is considering establishing a program to breed island gray foxes in captivity.

GAZELLE, DAMA
Gazella dama

PHYLUM: Chordata
CLASS: Mammalia
ORDER: Artiodactyla
FAMILY: Bovidae
STATUS: Endangered, IUCN
RANGE: Algeria, Chad, Libya, Mali, Mauritania, Morocco, Niger, Senegal, Sudan, Western Sahara

Gazelle, dama
Gazella dama

Description and biology

The dama gazelle, a graceful antelope found in the Sahara Desert region of Africa, has long legs, a long neck, and ringed horns curved back in the shape of a lyre (musical instrument). Its neck and a portion of its back are reddish brown in color, while the rest of its body is white (including one spot on the inside of its neck). An average dama gazelle has a head and body length of 40 to 67 inches (102 to 170 centimeters) and measures 35 to 42 inches (89 and 107 centimeters) high at its shoulder. Its tail, white with a black tip, extends 9 to 12 inches (23 to 30 centimeters). The animal weighs between 90 and 185 pounds (41 and 84 kilograms).

Like most species of gazelle, the dama gazelle has keen senses of hearing and smell. It grazes on shrubs and trees such as acacia and desert date. This gazelle travels alone or in small groups in search of food. A female dama gazelle gives birth usually to one infant after a gestation (pregnancy) period of 160 to 220 days.

A female dama gazelle nursing her young.

Habitat and current distribution

Once populous in the countries of Libya and Morocco, the dama gazelle is now virtually extinct in northern Africa. The animal currently ranges across several countries in central and western Africa. A few thousand are found in Mali, Chad, and Niger. Only very small and scattered populations survive in other African countries.

In its range, the dama gazelle inhabits the arid (dry) grassy zone between the Sahara and the Sahel (an semiarid area south of the Sahara). It prefers to live on stony or rocky terrain, especially around the edges of hills.

History and conservation measures

Like many other gazelle species, the dama gazelle is vanishing from its traditional range because of illegal hunting, habitat destruction, and competition for food from domestic livestock.

Although protected areas exist in the dama gazelle's range, such as the Ouadi Rime–Ouadi Achim Faunal Reserve in Chad and the Aïr and Ténère National Nature Reserve in Niger, they afford the animal little security. Illegal hunting, especially from motor vehicles, occurs inside and outside the reserves.

The need to feed an expanding human population also threatens the animals. Dama gazelle habitat is disappearing as irrigation and other agricultural methods have turned African deserts and grasslands into farmland. Facing competition from grazing livestock, dama gazelles have been forced to move south of their usual range in search of food. Such movement has brought the animals into even greater contact with humans. The result has been increased hunting.

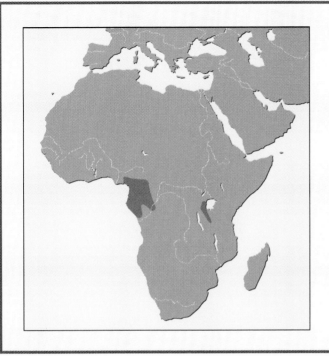

GORILLA
Gorilla gorilla

PHYLUM: Chordata
CLASS: Mammalia
ORDER: Primates
FAMILY: Hominidae
STATUS: Endangered, IUCN
Endangered, ESA
RANGE: Angola, Cameroon,
Central African Republic, Congo,
Congo Republic, Equatorial
Guinea, Gabon, Nigeria, Rwanda,
Uganda

Gorilla

Gorilla gorilla

Description and biology

The gorilla is considered the most intelligent land animal other than humans. It is the largest of the living primates, an order of mammals that includes lemurs, monkeys, chimpanzees, orangutans, and human beings. When standing on its hind legs, an average male gorilla measures 5 to 5.75 feet (1.5 to 1.75 meters) high. It can weigh between 300 and 500 pounds (136 and 227 kilograms). Females are smaller, measuring about 5 feet (1.5 meters) in height and weighing between 200 and 250 pounds (91 and 114 kilograms). The color of a gorilla's coat varies from brown–gray to black. In males, the hair on the back begins to turn silver after 10 years of age. Males also have a large bone on top of their skull (called the sagittal crest) that supports their massive jaw muscles and gives them their distinctive high

The largest of the living primates, gorillas are considered the most intelligent land mammals after humans.

forehead. Both sexes have small ears, broad nostrils, and a black, hairless face.

Gorillas are active during the day, foraging for a variety of vines, herbs, leaves, fruit, roots, and bark. During the wet season (April to June), the animals may move as little as 1,500 feet (457 meters) a day in search of food. During the dry season (July to August), they may travel almost 1 mile (1.6 kilometers). At night, gorillas build individual nests from branches and leaves in trees or on the ground.

Highly social animals, gorillas form groups of 5 to 10 members, although larger groups have been documented. An average group is composed of a dominant mature male (called a silverback) and several females and their young. When young males in the group become mature (at about age 11), they leave to form their own groups. Young females also leave upon reaching maturity (at about age 8), joining lone males or other groups.

Breeding between males and females can take place any time during the year. After a gestation period of 250 to 270 days, a female gorilla gives birth to a single infant. She will carry her infant for the first few months of its life, after which time it will begin to crawl and then walk. The young gorilla will remain dependent on its mother for up to three years. Almost half of all infant gorillas die. Female gorillas successfully raise only two to three young during their lives.

Scientists have recognized three subspecies of gorilla: the western lowland gorilla (*Gorilla gorilla gorilla*), the eastern lowland gorilla (*Gorilla gorilla graueri*), and the mountain gorilla (*Gorilla gorilla berengei*).

Habitat and current distribution

All three gorilla subspecies prefer forest habitats. The western lowland gorilla is found in Nigeria, Cameroon, Central African Republic, Río Muni (the portion of Equatorial Guinea on the African mainland), Gabon, Congo Republic, and Angola. Its population is estimated to be about 35,000. The eastern lowland gorilla, having a population between 3,000 and 5,000, is found primarily in eastern Congo. The mountain gorilla is found in the Virunga Mountains, a range of volcanic mountains stretching across eastern Congo, southwestern Uganda, and northwestern Rwanda. With a population of about 600, the mountain gorilla is the most endangered of the three gorilla subspecies.

History and conservation measures

Hunting has been the leading threat to gorillas for years. The animals are killed for use as food or trapped for use as pets. Although current international agreements ban the selling or trading of gorillas as pets, illegal capture of the animals continues.

As human populations swell in Africa, increasing numbers of gorillas are hunted for their meat, known as bush meat. A hunter can receive $30 for the remains of a 400–pound (180–kilogram) male gorilla. Female gorillas are also slaughtered, and their infants are captured and sold to private collectors or zoos. Sometimes hunters make more money for live infant gorillas than for the remains of dead adults.

The destruction of African forests is another serious threat to gorillas. More and more of their habitat has been cleared to create farms and to supply European and Asian timber companies. Logging roads, built deep into the forests, also allow hunters easy access to remaining gorillas.

African countries within the gorilla's range are trying to establish conservation programs for the animal. These efforts, though, are often thwarted by limited finances and social and political unrest. A successful program has been the Mountain Gorilla Veterinary Project, which provides health care for injured and sick mountain gorillas in Rwanda, Congo, and Uganda. It is one of the few programs in the world to provide treatment to an endangered species in its natural habitat.

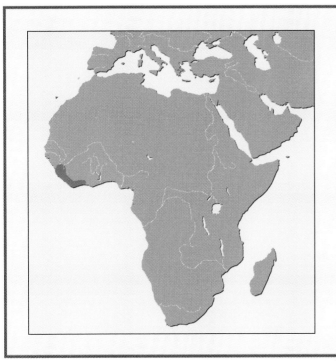

HIPPOPOTAMUS, PYGMY
Hexaprotodon liberiensis

PHYLUM: Chordata
CLASS: Mammalia
ORDER: Artiodactyla
FAMILY: Hippopotamidae
STATUS: Vulnerable, IUCN
RANGE: Côte d'Ivoire, Guinea, Guinea–Bissau, Liberia, Nigeria, Sierra Leone

Hippopotamus, pygmy
Hexaprotodon liberiensis

Description and biology

The pygmy hippopotamus is smaller and more piglike in appearance than its larger relative, the common hippopotamus. Its skin color is generally black, with a greenish tinge on the top of its back. Its belly is cream or yellow–gray. Its eyes are on the side of its round head instead of on top as in the common hippo. An average pygmy hippo has a head and body length of 5 to 5.5 feet (1.5 to 1.7 meters) and a shoulder height of 30 to 39 inches (76 to 99 centimeters). Its tail extends 6 inches (15 centimeters). It weighs between 355 and 600 pounds (161 and 272 kilograms). By contrast, an average common hippo weighs between 2,425 and 5,720 pounds (1,100 and 2,597 kilograms).

The pygmy hippo is a solitary animal, spending much of its time on the shore near swamps and rivers. It goes in the water only occasionally. Like the common hippo, the pygmy hippo has glands beneath its skin that secrete a pink, sweat–like substance. This biological fact has inspired the myth that hippos "sweat blood." This pink substance helps to regulate the hippo's skin temperature. Because its skin is sensitive to the sun, the pygmy hippo seeks shelter during the day in thickets and other forested areas. It feeds at night on leaves, shoots, grasses, roots, and fruits.

Male and female pygmy hippos usually mate in the water at any time during the year. After a gestation (pregnancy) period of 188 days, a female pygmy hippo gives birth to one calf. She then nurses that calf for eight months.

Habitat and current distribution

Pygmy hippos inhabit lowland forests. They are found in the tropical region of western Africa, primarily in the country of Liberia. Wildlife biologists (people who study living organisms) estimated that the pygmy hippo population in Liberia in the early 1980s was several thousand. No estimates have been made since then, but the population has almost certainly decreased.

History and conservation measures

Deforestation and hunting are the major threats to pygmy hippopotami. Africans hunt the animal and its larger relative for their meat and hides, which are used to make whips and shields. Very few conservation efforts exist for the pygmy hippopotamus. Between 350 and 400 pygmy hippos are held in captivity throughout the world.

HOG, PYGMY
Sus salvanius

PHYLUM: Chordata
CLASS: Mammalia
ORDER: Artiodactyla
FAMILY: Suidae
STATUS: Critically endangered, IUCN
Endangered, ESA
RANGE: Bhutan, India, Nepal

Hog, pygmy
Sus salvanius

Description and biology

The pygmy hog is the smallest of all pig species. An average adult pygmy hog is 25 inches (63.5 centimeters) long, stands 10 inches (25 centimeters) tall at its shoulder, and weighs 19 pounds (8.6 kilograms). Its short tail measures only 1 inch (2.5 centimeters). Its hide is covered with coarse dark brown or black bristles. Because of its small, bullet–like shape, the animal is extremely agile.

Male pygmy hogs are larger than their female counterparts and have exposed tusks. The normally solitary males interact with the females only during mating season. A female pygmy hog gives birth to a litter of two to six infants, usually in late April or May, after a gestation (pregnancy) period of about 100 days. Both males and females build and use their nests throughout the year.

Habitat and current distribution

Pygmy hogs inhabit dense, tall grasslands. They are found primarily in two wildlife sanctuaries in northwestern Assam (a state in far eastern India): Manas Wildlife Sanctuary and Barnadi Wildlife Sanctuary. Scientists estimate the total number of pygmy hogs to be no more than 300. The actual number may be far less.

History and conservation measures

The pygmy hog is one of the most endangered mammals in the world. Destruction of the animal's habitat is the main reason. Farmers routinely set fire to grassland forests to clear them for agricultural use. Many pygmy hogs are killed because they cannot escape the extensive fires. Those that do escape are forced onto very small grassland areas where they are

The pygmy hog is one of the most endangered mammals on Earth because of habitat loss. If this habitat loss continues, the pygmy hog will probably face extinction soon.

sometimes killed by unexpected fires or onto tea plantations where they are often killed by hunters.

The international wildlife community and the Indian government have focused much attention on the pygmy hog's plight. In 1985, the International Union for Conservation of Nature and Natural Resources (IUCN) placed the pygmy hog on its first list of the 12 most threatened species in the world. The Indian government has given the animal the maximum legal protection allowed under its Indian Wild Life Protection Act. In 1986, the United Nations Educational, Scientific, and Cultural Organization (UNESCO) designated the Manas Wildlife Sanctuary as a World Heritage Site.

All these measures have done little to stop the destruction of pygmy hog habitat. If grassland fires in their habitat are allowed to continue unchecked, pygmy hogs will face extinction.

HORSE, PRZEWALSKI'S
Equus przewalskii

PHYLUM: Chordata
CLASS: Mammalia
ORDER: Perissodactyla
FAMILY: Equidae
STATUS: Extinct in the wild, IUCN
Endangered, ESA
RANGE: China, Kazakhstan, Mongolia

Horse, Przewalski's

Equus przewalskii

Description and biology

Przewalski's horse is the last truly wild horse. Slightly smaller than most domestic horses, it has a compact body with a thick neck and large head. The color of its upper body is dun (a dull grayish brown), while its belly and muzzle are much lighter. The horse has a dark stripe along its backbone and a dark, plumed tail. The dark hair on its head and along its neck (the mane) is short and stands erect. Unlike the domestic horse, Przewalski's horse sheds its mane and the short hairs at the base of its tail annually.

An average Przewalski's horse may reach 8 feet (2.4 meters) in length and stand 4 to 4.5 feet (1.2 to 1.4 meters) high at its shoulders. It may vary in weight between 440 and 750 pounds (200 and 340 kilograms). The horse feeds primarily on grass and other low vegetation.

Przewalski's horse is considered extinct in the wild since there are no genetically pure specimans remaining.

Groups of Przewalski's horses are headed by a dominant stallion (male), which is responsible for breeding with most of the group's females. The females usually give birth to a single foal (infant) between April and June, after a gestation (pregnancy) period of 330 to 340 days. The foals may nurse for up to two years.

Habitat and current distribution

Przewalski's horses prefer open grassland, steppe (vast, semiarid grass–covered plain), and semidesert areas. The last possible sighting of Przewalski's horse in the wild was in 1968. Chinese biologists (people who study living organisms) believe there may be a small population of horses inhabiting northeastern Xingiang (an autonomous region in northwestern China). It is more likely that this group is extinct.

Over 1,000 Przewalski's horses are currently held in captivity in zoos and reserves around the world.

History and conservation measures

Przewalski's horse was discovered in 1878 by Russian geographer and explorer Nikolai Mikhailovich Przhevalsky (1839–1888). Scientists believe the horse once ranged from western Mongolia to northern Xingiang and western Kazakhstan.

By 1900, hunting and competition with domestic horses for food and water greatly reduced the Przewalski's horse population. By the 1950s, the remaining animals were seen in a small area between southwestern Mongolia and northwestern China called the Takhin–Shara–Nuru (mountain of the yellow horses). Przewalski's horses have interbred with feral horses (wild horses descended from domestic horses) over the years to such an extent that scientists believe no genetically pure Przewalski's horse currently exists in the wild.

In June 1994, a small herd of Przewalski's horses that was bred in captivity was returned to the wild in Mongolia. The horses were kept in large enclosures for two years while they adjusted to the harsh climate. The herd is flourishing and is expected to reach a self–sustaining population by the year 2000.

HYENA, BROWN
Hyaena Brunnea

PHYLUM: Chordata
CLASS: Mammalia
ORDER: Carnivora
FAMILY: Hyaenidae
STATUS: Endangered, ESA
RANGE: Angola, Botswana, Mozambique, Namibia, South Africa, Zimbabwe

Hyena, brown

Hyaena Brunnea

Description and biology

The brown hyena, also known as the strand wolf, has a long, brown, shaggy coat with lighter underparts. Its face and legs are gray to black. An average brown hyena measures 43 to 53 inches (109 to 135 centimeters) long and stands 25 to 35 inches (64 to 89 centimeters) high at its shoulder. It weighs between 82 and 104 pounds (37 and 47 kilograms). Males are larger than females.

The brown hyena feeds primarily on the remains of prey killed by other predators. With its strong teeth and jaws, the animal can crush and eat bone. It also feeds on insects, eggs, fruits, and an occasional small animal or bird that it kills. Although it has acute vision and hearing, the brown hyena locates its prey by scent. Lions and spotted hyenas are the animal's main predators.

Brown hyenas sleep during the day and hunt at dusk or during the night. While on its nightly hunting expedition, a brown hyena will normally cover about 19 square miles (49 square kilometers). Some have been known to travel over 31 square miles (80 square kilometers).

Although often solitary in their habits, brown hyenas will form clans of up to 10 members. Male and female brown hyenas mate at any time during the year. After a gestation (pregnancy) period of 90 to 100 days, a female will give birth to 1 to 5 cubs. In a communal den (shared by all members in a clan), cubs may suckle from females other than their mother. All members of the clan help to feed the cubs by carrying food to the den.

Brown hyenas are often killed because of the false belief that they are a threat to livestock.

Habitat and current distribution

In southern Africa, brown hyenas inhabit arid (dry) areas such as rocky deserts with thick brush, open grassland and scrub (land covered with stunted trees and shrubs), and semi-deserts. They sleep in dense vegetation, under sheltering rocks, or in burrows dug by other animals.

History and conservation measures

Scientists do not know the exact number of existing brown hyenas, but they believe the animals' range and population has been greatly reduced. Of the six African countries where brown hyenas can be found, only Botswana and Zimbabwe host sizable populations.

Many humans dislike brown hyenas because of their foul stench and their cry (which sounds like maniacal laughter). Brown hyenas are often killed by humans for these reasons and because the animals are seen as a threat to livestock. Since brown hyenas feed on carrion (decaying flesh of dead animals), this last view is utterly false.

Brown hyenas are given protection in several conservation areas in the Kalahari, an arid plateau region stretching about 100,000 square miles (259,000 square kilometers) in Botswana, Namibia, and South Africa. The animals are also protected along the coastal regions of the southern Namib Desert in western Namibia.

JAGUAR
Panthera onca

PHYLUM: Chordata
CLASS: Mammalia
ORDER: Carnivora
FAMILY: Felidae
STATUS: Lower risk: near threatened, IUCN Endangered, ESA
RANGE: Argentina, Belize, Bolivia, Brazil, Colombia, Costa Rica, Ecuador, French Guiana, Guatemala, Guyana, Honduras, Mexico, Nicaragua, Panama, Paraguay, Peru, Suriname, Venezuela

Jaguar
Panthera onca

Description and biology

The jaguar is the largest living member of the cat family in North and South America and the third largest in the world. Its coat ranges from yellow–brown to auburn and is covered with black spots and rosettes, or rings, encircling spots. An average adult jaguar has a head and body length of 4 to 6 feet (1.2 to 1.8 meters) and a tail length of 18 to 30 inches (46 to 76 centimeters). It stands about 2.5 feet (0.7 meter) high at its shoulder and weighs between 100 and 250 pounds (45 and 115 kilograms). Of the big cats, only the jaguar and the snow leopard do not seem to roar.

Jaguars are good swimmers, runners, and tree climbers. Their diet includes fish, frogs, turtles, small alligators, iguanas, peccaries (mammals related to the pig), monkeys, birds,

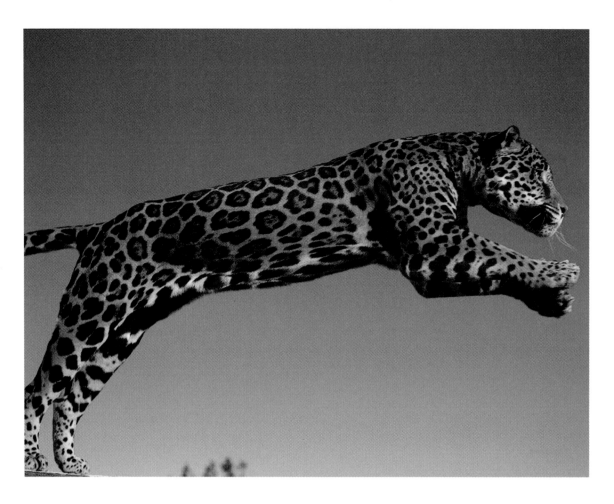

A jaguar leaping for its prey. Jaguars are good runners, swimmers, and tree climbers.

deer, dogs, and cattle. Jaguars are solitary mammals and are quick to defend their chosen hunting territory. For male jaguars, this territory ranges between 8 and 80 square miles (20 and 207 square kilometers); for females, it ranges between 4 and 27 square miles (10 and 70 square kilometers).

Male and female jaguars come together only to mate. In tropical areas, mating takes place at any time during the year. In areas with cooler climates, jaguars mate in the spring. After a gestation (pregnancy) period of 90 to 110 days, a female jaguar gives birth to a litter of one to four cubs. She raises the cubs on her own, and they may stay with her for up to two years.

Habitat and current distribution

Jaguars are found in parts of Mexico, Central America, and South America as far south as northern Argentina. Because the animals are secretive and rare, biologists (people who study living organisms) have not been able to determine the exact number remaining in the wild. The largest remaining population of jaguars is believed to live in the Amazonian rain forest.

Jaguars live in a variety of habitats, including tropical and subtropical forests, open woodlands, mangroves, swamps, scrub thickets, and savannas.

History and conservation measures

The jaguar once inhabited areas as far north as the southern United States. It is now extinct over much of its former range. The primary reason for the animal's decline was ruthless hunting, both for sport and for the jaguar's prized coat. In the early to mid–1960s, spotted cat skins were in great demand. International treaties have all but eliminated the commercial trade of cat pelts.

Jaguars now face the threat of habitat destruction. The clearing of forests to build ranches and farms has rapidly eliminated the animals' original habitat. Forced to live next to farmland, jaguars are often killed by farmers because they prey on domestic animals.

Small populations of jaguars are protected in large national parks in Bolivia, Brazil, Colombia, Peru, and Venezuela. Smaller reserves and private ranches in these areas provide protection to isolated pairs or families. The jaguar has been bred successfully in zoos.

KANGAROO RAT, GIANT
Dipodomys ingens

PHYLUM: Chordata
CLASS: Mammalia
ORDER: Rodentia
FAMILY: Heteromyidae
STATUS: Critically endangered, IUCN
Endangered, ESA
RANGE: USA (California)

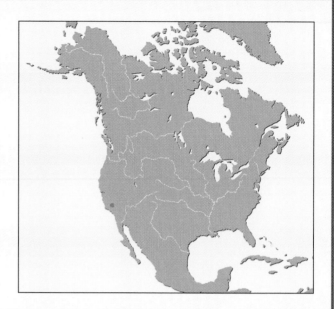

Kangaroo rat, giant
Dipodomys ingens

Description and biology

The kangaroo rat, a desert rodent related to the pocket mouse, is so–named because it uses its long legs and tail to leap like a kangaroo. There are about 20 kangaroo rat species, the largest of which is the giant kangaroo rat. This species can have a head and body length of up to 14 inches (36 centimeters) and weigh up to 6 ounces (170 grams). Its tail can measure up to 8 inches (20 centimeters) long. The animal has a mouselike head, large eyes, and cheek pouches in which it stores food. Its body is covered with long, silky fur that is pale brown above and white underneath. Its tail ends in a tuft of black–and–white hair.

The giant kangaroo rat eats seeds, leaves, stems, and buds of young plants. Like other desert animals, the kangaroo rat seldom drinks water, but obtains the moisture it needs from the food it eats. It also conserves the water it takes in by foraging only at night.

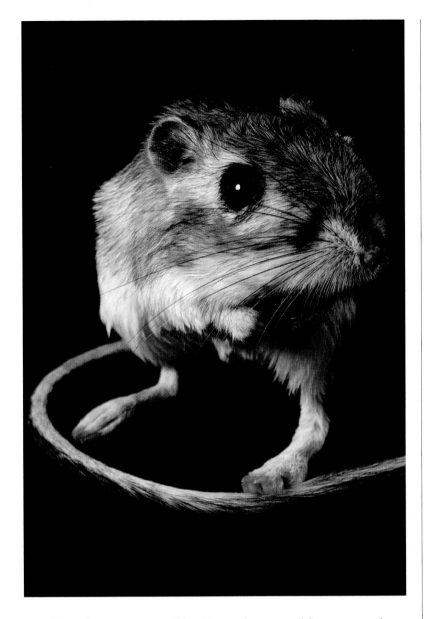

Giant kangaroo rats live in underground burrows, where they store food for the winter months. The normally solitary male and female kangaroo rats come together only to mate, which may occur at any time during the year. After a gestation (pregnancy) period of about 30 days, a female giant kangaroo rat gives birth to a litter of two to five young.

Habitat and current distribution

The giant kangaroo rat is now restricted to a grassland area of less than 5 square miles (13 square kilometers) between the Carrizo Plain and the city of Taft in southwestern California.

History and conservation measures

The giant kangaroo rat, like all kangaroo rat species, is threatened by habitat destruction due to a growing human population. Its former habitat has been turned into farmland, oil fields, or residential areas. The animal also faces the risks of pesticide poisoning (from overspraying on nearby farms) and attacks by domestic cats.

Conservationists are trying to obtain land in Kern and San Luis Obispo Counties in southwestern California in order to save suitable habitat for the giant kangaroo rat.

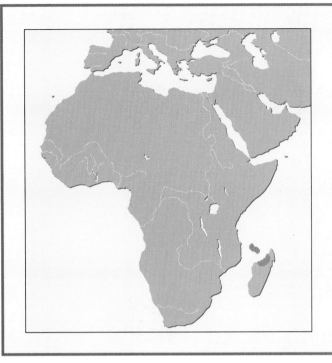

LEMUR, MONGOOSE
Eulemur mongoz

PHYLUM: Chordata
CLASS: Mammalia
ORDER: Primates
FAMILY: Lemuridae
STATUS: Vulnerable, IUCN
Endangered, ESA
RANGE: Comoros, Madagascar

Lemur, mongoose

Eulemur mongoz

Description and biology

Lemurs are mammals with monkey–like bodies and limbs. They're found only on Madagascar (large island lying in the Indian Ocean off the eastern coast of the African country of Mozambique) and adjacent islands. The mongoose lemur is one of only two lemur species found on both Madagascar and Comoros (group of islands between northeastern Mozambique and northwestern Madagascar). It is covered with long, soft fur and has a ruff (projecting growth of fur) around its neck and ears. The upper bodies of male mongoose lemurs are gray in color. The mongoose lemur has a pale face with bushy, reddish brown cheeks. The upper bodies of females are gray–brown. They have a dark face with bushy, white cheeks. Both sexes are white underneath.

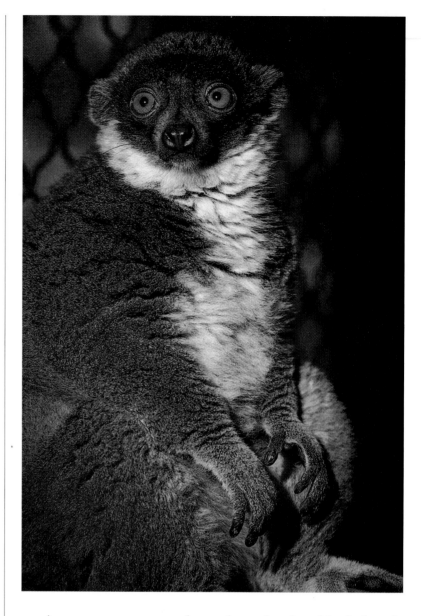

An average mongoose lemur has a head and body length of 12 to 17 inches (30 to 43 centimeters) and weighs 4.5 to 6.6 pounds (2 to 3 kilograms). The tail of the mongoose lemur is longer than its body, extending 16 to 25 inches (40 to 64 centimeters).

Mongoose lemurs are active either at night or during the day, depending on the season and area. Their diet is mainly composed of flowers, fruit, and leaves. Family groups are made up of a male, a female, and their infants. Female mongoose lemurs normally give birth to one infant in mid–October after a gestation (pregnancy) period of 128 to 135 days.

Habitat and current distribution

The mongoose lemur inhabits dry deciduous (shedding plants and trees) forests on northwestern Madagascar and humid forests on the Comoros islands of Anjouan and Mohéli. The lemurs on the Comoros are probably descendants of lemurs brought to the islands by fishermen from Madagascar.

History and conservation measures

Biologists (people who study living organisms) believe the number of mongoose lemurs in existence is declining. In Madagascar, the animals are found only in the protected area of Ankarafantsika. The reserve, however, is not well managed to provide protection for the wildlife it harbors. Nearby residents are continually clearing forested land around (and even within) the reserve to obtain lumber and to create agricultural land for livestock and crops.

On the islands of the Comoros, laws have been passed to protect the mongoose lemurs, but little has been done to enforce them. An increase in the number of cyclones (violent windstorms) that have hit the islands recently has also taken its toll on the animals.

LEOPARD
Panthera pardus

PHYLUM: Chordata
CLASS: Mammalia
ORDER: Carnivora
FAMILY: Felidae
STATUS: Endangered, ESA
Threatened, ESA (parts of Africa)
RANGE: Africa (south of the Sahara Desert), southeastern Asia

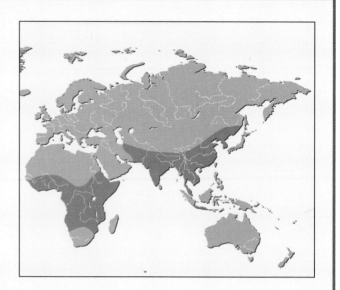

Leopard
Panthera pardus

Description and biology

A large member of the cat family, the leopard is known for its light to tawny brown coat patterned with black spots and rosettes, or rings. Unlike those of the jaguar, the rosettes of the leopard never have spots inside them. Some leopards are born with a black coat that still has the characteristic spotting. Found mainly in southern Asia, these cats are commonly (but incorrectly) called black panthers. An average leopard has a head and body length of 38 to 75 inches (97 to 191 centimeters) and weighs 65 to 155 pounds (30 to 70 kilograms). Its tail can reach a length of up to 3 feet (1 meter).

Leopards are solitary mammals that hunt primarily at night. Their diet includes monkeys and other small mammals, birds, rodents, and insects. Good climbers, leopards often store

Because of the demand for leopard fur, the animals are often illegally hunted. It is this hunting that has lead to the leopard's endangered status.

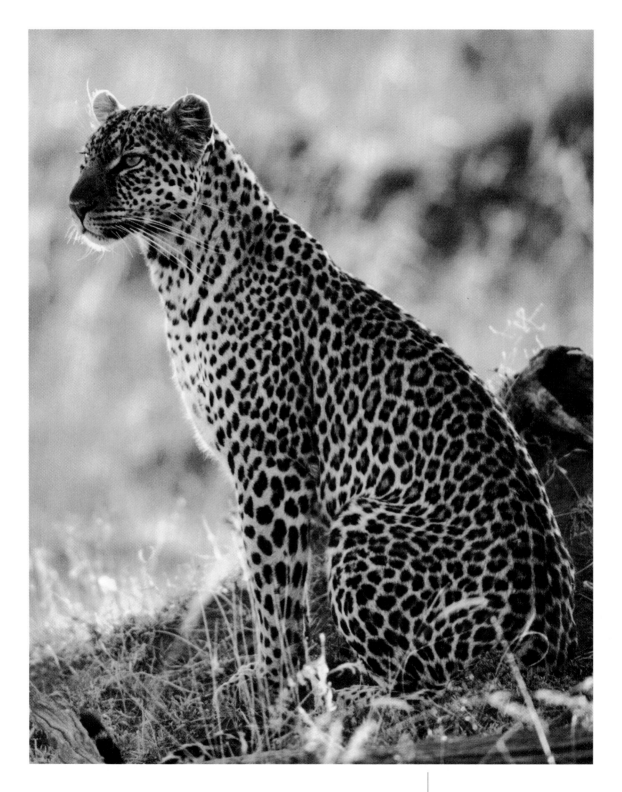

their dead prey in trees. They cover a home range of about 4 to 20 square miles (10 to 51 square kilometers) in search of food.

Male and female leopards come together only to mate, which can occur at any time during the year. After a gestation (pregnancy) period of 90 to 105 days, a female leopard gives birth to a litter of three to five cubs. She alone cares for the cubs, hiding them until they are six to eight weeks old. The young leopards nurse for several months and may stay with the mother for 18 to 20 months.

Habitat and current distribution

Leopards have the ability to adapt to almost any environment. As long as prey is available, these cats inhabit areas ranging from semidesert to dense rain forest. They are found in Africa south of the Sahara Desert and in southeastern Asia.

Leopards are considered endangered throughout their range. The only exception is the region south of the African countries of Gabon, Congo, Congo Republic, Uganda, and Kenya. Because leopards are more numerous here, they are considered only threatened.

History and conservation measures

Like most spotted cats, the leopard has been a victim of the fur trade. Although global treaties protect the leopard, poachers still hunt the animal to sell on the international market. In Africa, it is legal to hunt leopards for sport.

Contact between humans and leopards has not favored the animals. As more and more of their habitat has been converted to farm and ranch land, leopards have been forced to prey on domestic livestock. In response, farmers and ranchers have actively sought to poison the animals.

Leopards have protection only in national parks, where they are considered a tourist attraction.

LEOPARD, SNOW
Panthera uncia

PHYLUM: Chordata
CLASS: Mammalia
ORDER: Carnivora
FAMILY: Felidae
STATUS: Endangered, IUCN
Endangered, ESA
RANGE: Afghanistan, Bhutan,
China, India, Kazakhstan,
Kyrgyzstan, Mongolia, Nepal,
Pakistan, Russia, Tajikistan,
Uzbekistan

Leopard, snow
Panthera uncia

Description and biology

The snow leopard, or ounce, has a beautiful coat of long, pale gray fur with white underneath. Its coat is patterned with solid black spots on its head and legs and dark gray rosettes (rings) on the rest of its body. The animal is smaller than its closest relative, the leopard. An average snow leopard has a head and body length of 48 to 56 inches (122 to 142 centimeters) and weighs 132 to 165 pounds (60 to 75 kilograms). Its heavy, thickly furred tail measures 32 to 40 inches (81 to 102 centimeters). The snow leopard has thick chest muscles for climbing and large, heavily padded forepaws for walking through snow. An excellent leaper, the animal can jump as far as 50 feet (15 meters) in a single bound.

Snow leopards usually hunt at dusk or at night. While their preferred prey is the bharal (a goatlike mammal), they also hunt yak, marmots, musk deer, and domestic livestock.

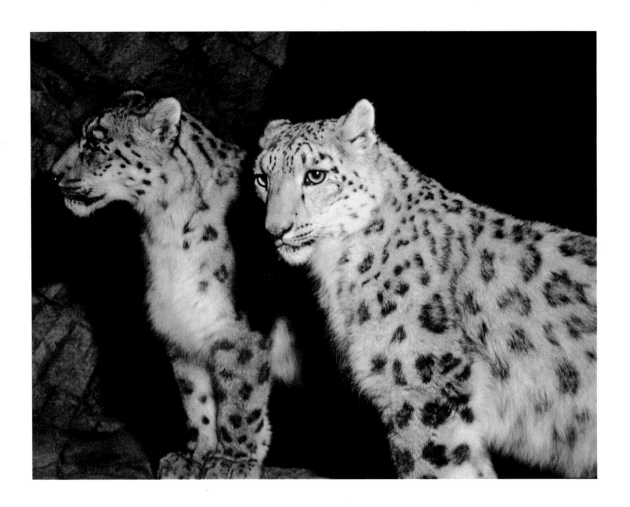

Two snow leopards from the Cincinnati Zoo. Unless the animals' natural habitat is preserved, they may fall victim to extinction.

An individual snow leopard's home range extends from 5 to 15 square miles (13 to 39 square kilometers).

Like other big cats, snow leopards are solitary animals. Males and females come together only to mate in late winter. After a gestation (pregnancy) period of 98 to 103 days, a female snow leopard gives birth to one to four cubs. The cubs nurse for at least two months and remain dependent on their mother for up to a year.

Habitat and current distribution

Snow leopards inhabit mountain ranges in central Asia. Their entire range covers a massive area of almost 1,000,000 square miles (2,590,000 square kilometers). However, these rare and endangered animals sparsely populate this area. Biologists (people who study living organisms) estimate that fewer than 5,000 snow leopards exist in the wild.

Snow leopards are normally found in dry alpine and sub-alpine regions above 9,840 feet (3,000 meters). During summer months, when their prey moves to higher pastures, snow leopards may climb to an altitude of 13,000 feet (3,960 meters).

History and conservation measures

Along with other spotted cats, the snow leopard has long been hunted for its prized coat. Although current international treaties protect the animal, poachers still hunt down the snow leopard and sell it illegally. Because some of the animal's habitat is not easy to reach, officials have a difficult time enforcing the snow leopard's protective rights.

Snow leopards are also threatened by human development. As human populations have grown in the region and snow leopard habitat has been converted into agricultural land for livestock, the animal's traditional prey has become scarce. Forced to feed on domestic animals, the snow leopard has become a target for angry farm and ranch owners.

Unless large areas of its natural habitat are preserved, the continued existence of the snow leopard is in jeopardy.

MANATEE, WEST INDIAN
Trichechus manatus

PHYLUM: Chordata

CLASS: Mammalia

ORDER: Sirenia

FAMILY: Trichechidae

STATUS: Vulnerable, IUCN Endangered, ESA

RANGE: Bahamas, Belize, Brazil, Colombia, Costa Rica, Cuba, Dominican Republic, French Guiana, Guatemala, Guyana, Haiti, Honduras, Jamaica, Mexico, Nicaragua, Panama, Puerto Rico, Suriname, Trinidad and Tobago, USA (Florida), Venezuela

Manatee, West Indian
Trichechus manatus

Description and biology

The West Indian manatee, also known as the Florida manatee, is a large marine mammal with a rounded, heavy gray body and a horizontally flattened tail. An average West Indian manatee has a combined body and tail length of 8 to 13 feet (2.4 to 4 meters) and weighs 800 to 3,500 pounds (360 to 1,590 kilograms). It has small eyes and no ear pinnas (external flaplike portions). The animal's nostrils are on the upper surface of its snout and can be tightly closed by valves when the manatee is underwater. Manatees often rest just below the water's surface, coming up to breathe every 15 or 20 minutes. They use their flexible flippers almost like hands for eating, moving through seagrass, touching, holding a nursing calf, and even hugging other manatees.

The manatee is the only marine mammal that feeds solely on vegetation. It eats a variety of aquatic plants, including water hyacinths, hydrillas, and seagrasses. The manatee is often called a sea cow because it grazes on marine seagrass meadows. It uses its split upper lip to grasp food and pull it into its mouth. Primarily a nocturnal (at night) feeder, the animal can consume up to 100 pounds (45 kilograms) of food a day.

Manatees have no particular breeding season, but most births seem to occur in spring and early summer. After a gestation (pregnancy) period of 13 months, a female manatee gives birth to one calf, which is about 4 feet (1.2 meters) long and weighs 60 pounds (27 kilograms). Even though it begins grazing on vegetation within a few months, the calf continues to nurse from its mother for one to two years.

Habitat and current distribution

The West Indian manatee is found in the coastal waters and rivers of Florida, Central America, and the West Indies. It prefers to inhabit slow–moving rivers, river mouths, bays, lagoons, coves, and other shallow coastal areas. It is at home in all types of water environments: fresh, brackish (slightly salty), and salt. The manatee requires warm water and will migrate great distances between winter and summer grounds.

The total number of West Indian manatees in existence is unknown, but a statewide survey in Florida in early 1997 listed the manatee population there at just over 2,220.

History and conservation measures

Native Americans hunted manatees for centuries, using the animals' flesh, bones (for medicine), and hide (for leather). When Spanish explorers began colonizing Caribbean islands in the sixteenth century, manatee hunting increased. Biologists (people who study living organisms) believe this hunting is responsible for the manatee's initial decline.

Natural events, such as sudden changes in water temperature, also can be deadly to manatees. In the 1980s, three abnormally cold winters in Florida lowered water temperatures throughout the state. In water below 60°F (15°C), manatees become sluggish, stop eating, and eventually die. Many manatees perished during those cold Florida winters.

The greatest continued threat to manatees, however, comes from humans. Many manatees drown each year from being trapped in fishing nets. Others are drowned or crushed by flood gates or canal locks. Some are injured by discarded fishing lines, hooks, and trash. The majority of manatee deaths in Florida are caused by collisions with speeding boats. Those animals that survive such collisions bear lifelong propeller scars.

In 1978, the Florida legislature passed the Florida Manatee Sanctuary Act, which designated the entire state a refuge and sanctuary for the animal. Manatee protection zones have been established in which boats are required to reduce their speed. In areas declared manatee refuges, no boats, swimmers, or divers are allowed. In other countries in the West Indian manatee's range, public education programs have been launched to raise awareness about the animal's plight.

MANDRILL
Mandrillus sphinx

PHYLUM: Chordata

CLASS: Mammalia

ORDER: Primates

FAMILY: Cercopithecidae

STATUS: Lower risk: near threatened, IUCN Endangered, ESA

RANGE: Cameroon, Congo Republic, Equatorial Guinea, Gabon

Mandrill

Mandrillus sphinx

Description and biology

Related to the baboon, the mandrill is the largest member of the monkey family. An average male has a head and body length of 31 inches (79 centimeters), a shoulder height of 20 inches (51 centimeters), and a tail length of 3 inches (8 centimeters). It weighs 119 pounds (54 kilograms). Females are considerably smaller.

Male mandrills are considered the most colorful of all mammals. While the animal's body fur is mainly dark brown, its bare areas (face and buttocks) are dazzlingly colored. Bright blue ridges line its face on either side of its nose. Its doglike muzzle is bright red. Black fur surrounds its close–set, yellow–brown eyes. Its beard and the edges of its mane are pale yellow. The pads on its buttocks are bright red, blue, and purple. The coloring on females and infants is not as brilliant.

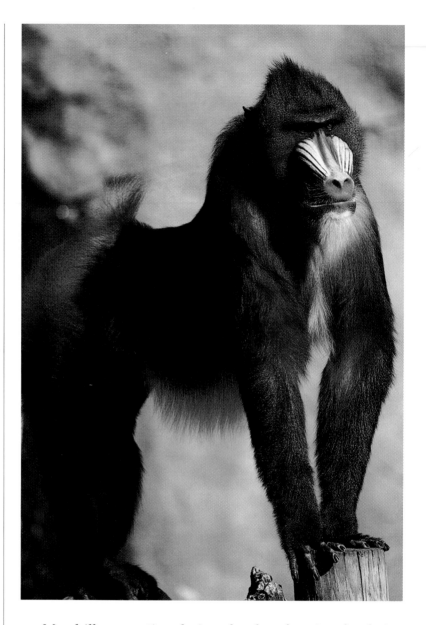

The most colorful of all mammals, the mandrill is the largest member of the primate family.

Mandrills are active during the day, foraging for fruits, buds, leaves, roots, insects, fungus, and seeds. When food is scarce, the animals sometimes raid crops from nearby farms and plantations. At night, they sleep in trees.

Social animals, mandrills form groups of 20 to 40 members headed by a single male. The home range of a single group may be between 12 and 19 square miles (31 and 48 square kilometers). Little is known about the mandrill's reproductive habits. Most female mandrills give birth between December and April after a gestation (pregnancy) period of about 170 days.

Habitat and current distribution

Mandrills are found in the tropical forests and thick bush areas south of the Sanaga River in southwestern Cameroon, Rí Muni (the portion of Equatorial Guinea on the African mainland), western Gabon, and southwestern Congo Republic.

Since mandrills avoid contact with humans, they are difficult to observe in the wild. Biologists (people who study living organisms) are, therefore, unsure of the total number currently in existence.

History and conservation measures

The mandrill population has drastically declined in the late twentieth century due to habitat destruction and hunting. It is relatively easy to hunt mandrills because they emit loud calls. Hunters sometimes use dogs to chase the animals up trees before shooting them down.

Local people hunt the mandrill for food in all countries in its range. Much of the animal's forest habitat has been logged for its timber or cleared to create farmland. Although the animal is found in several reserves, including the Campo Reserve in Cameroon and the large Lopé Okanda Reserve in Gabon, it receives little protection. Hunting, logging, and the building of settlements still take place within many of these areas. In Rí Muni, the mandrill receives no protection and is considered extremely rare.

MARKHOR
Capra falconeri

PHYLUM: Chordata
CLASS: Mammalia
ORDER: Artiodactyla
FAMILY: Bovidae
STATUS: Endangered, IUCN
Endangered, ESA
RANGE: Afghanistan, India,
Pakistan, Tajikistan, Turkmenistan,
Uzbekistan

Markhor
Capra falconeri

Description and biology

The markhor is one of the largest members of the goat family. An average markhor has a head and body length of 55 to 70 inches (140 to 195 centimeters) and a shoulder height of 26 to 40 inches (66 to 102 centimeters). Its tail measures 3 to 5.5 inches (8 to 14 centimeters). The animal may weigh between 70 and 240 pounds (30 and 110 kilograms). Males are substantially larger than females.

Male markhors have unique corkscrew–shaped horns that are very thick and heavy. They also have a large beard and a long, shaggy mane at the base of their neck. If a female has a beard, which is rare, it is small. The coat of both sexes varies in length and color with the seasons. In summer, a markhor's coat is short and reddish brown. In winter, it is long, silky, and gray.

Markhors are active during the day, grazing on grasses and herbs or browsing (feeding on the tender shoots, twigs, and leaves) on shrubs and low trees. Wolves, leopards, and snow leopards often prey on the markhor.

Males generally live by themselves, while females and young live in groups of 10 to 12. During the winter mating season, males compete with each other over the right to mate with females. After a gestation (pregnancy) period of about 155 days, a female markhor gives birth to one or two young.

Habitat and current distribution

Markhors inhabit rocky areas, open forested slopes, and meadows in the rugged mountains of central Asia. Their range extends from the western end of the Himalayas in northwestern India to southern Tajikistan and Uzbekistan.

There are three subspecies of the markhor: the Kabal markhor (*Capra falconeri megaceros*), the straight–horned markhor (*Capra falconeri jerdoni*), and the Tajik markhor (*Capra falconeri heptneri*). Kabal and straight–horn markhors are found primarily in Afghanistan and Pakistan. Tajik markhors occupy southern Uzbekistan and Tajikistan. With population numbers ranging from 700 to just over 3,000, all three subspecies are in danger of extinction.

History and conservation measures

Excessive hunting, primarily for the markhor's horns, is the main reason for the animal's decline. As the human population increases in the markhor's range, so does the destruction of its habitat. Trees are cut down for timber, forested land is cleared to create agricultural land, and domestic sheep and goats compete with the markhor for food.

Twenty–seven protected areas have been established in the markhor's range. The level of safety in these areas, however, is limited by political unrest and military activity in the region. In addition, most markhor populations are very small and often isolated from each other, making conservation efforts difficult.

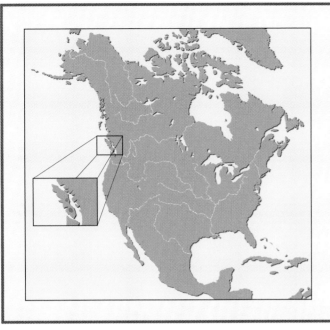

MARMOT, VANCOUVER ISLAND
Marmota vancouverensis

PHYLUM: Chordata
CLASS: Mammalia
ORDER: Rodentia
FAMILY: Sciuridae
STATUS: Endangered, IUCN
Endangered, ESA
RANGE: Canada (Vancouver Island)

Marmot, Vancouver Island

Marmota vancouverensis

Description and biology

Marmots are ground–living rodents of the squirrel family, closely related to the chipmunk, ground squirrel, and prairie dog. The woodchuck is the best–known North American marmot species. The Vancouver Island marmot has coarse fur and a bushy tail 4 to 10 inches (10 to 25 centimeters) long. Its deep brown coat is darker than that of most marmots. An average Vancouver Island marmot has a head and body length of 12 to 23.5 inches (30 to 60 centimeters) and weighs between 6.5 and 16.5 pounds (3 and 7.5 kilograms).

Vancouver Island marmots feed on plants, especially the flowering parts. They hibernate for six to nine months in a den, huddled together in a family group of about eight members. Male and female Vancouver Island marmots mate after emerging from hibernation, usually in April or May. After a gestation (pregnancy) period of four to five weeks, a female marmot gives birth to a litter of two to six young.

113

Habitat and current distribution

This species of marmot is found only on Vancouver Island, off the southwest coast of British Columbia, Canada. It inhabits the higher regions of the coastal mountains that mark the central and southern parts of the island. Most of the known groups of marmots are found in a small area between Green Mountain and Butler Peak in the island's southern section. In the mid–1980s, biologists (people who study living organisms) estimated that the population of Vancouver Island marmots numbered 231.

The marmots prefer to inhabit steep, rocky slopes and open meadows at elevations between 3,280 and 6,560 feet (1,000 and 2,000 meters).

History and conservation measures

The Vancouver Island marmot was discovered in 1911. Since that time, its population has declined, probably as a result of contact with humans. Extensive logging and the building of recreation areas such as ski resorts have destroyed some marmot habitat. Hunting of the animal, more common in the past, continues even today.

The Vancouver Island Marmot Preservation Society has led recent conservation efforts to save the animal. The organization has spurred the Canadian government to conduct scientific field research on the species and to establish captive breeding programs, among other actions. The society's efforts have been successful. The population of Vancouver Island marmots has increased since the 1970s.

MONKEY, CENTRAL AMERICAN SQUIRREL
Saimiri oerstedii

PHYLUM: Chordata
CLASS: Mammalia
ORDER: Primates
FAMILY: Cebidae
STATUS: Endangered, IUCN
Endangered, ESA
RANGE: Costa Rica, Panama

Monkey, Central American squirrel
Saimiri oerstedii

Description and biology

The Central American squirrel monkey is also known as the red–backed squirrel monkey because of the short, thick reddish fur covering its back, limbs, and tail. The fur on the rest of its body, including its face, is white. An average Central American squirrel monkey has a head and body length of 9 to 14 inches (23 to 36 centimeters) and weighs between 1 and 2.4 pounds (0.5 and 1.1 kilograms). The tail, which is not prehensile (adapted for grasping or holding by wrapping around something), measures 14 to 18 inches (36 to 46 centimeters) long.

The Central American squirrel monkey spends most of its time in trees and feeds on fruit and insects. Groups of 10 to 40 monkeys live together, often combining with other groups to form very large societies. Some groups inhabit forest areas as small as 2 acres (0.8 hectare). Others may occupy as much as 50 to 100 acres (20 to 40 hectares).

A female Central American squirrel monkey with her baby. The infant will remain with its mother for almost a year.

Males often fight with each other over the right to mate with a female. After a gestation (pregnancy) period of 152 to 170 days, a female Central American squirrel monkey gives birth to a single infant. It clings to its mother after birth and remains dependent on her for almost a year.

Habitat and current distribution

Central American squirrel monkeys are found only in western panama and southern Costa Rica. Biologists (people who study living organisms) have estimated that the Costa Rican population numbers 3,000. The number of monkeys living in Panama is unknown. In these two regions, the animals prefer to inhabit forests, woodlands, and areas dominated by shrubs and low, bushy trees.

History and conservation measures

The population of Central American squirrel monkeys has decreased greatly since the 1950s. The primary reason is due to deforestation (the loss of forests as they are rapidly cut down to produce timber or to make land available for agriculture). Much of the squirrel monkey's habitat has been converted to banana plantations, cattle ranches, and rice and sugar cane farms.

Costa Rican farmers have transformed this land through slash–and–burn agriculture, a process whereby a forest is cut down and all trees and vegetation are burned to create cleared land. Although this process clears land quickly, it robs the soil of essential nutrients. The land does not stay fertile for very long. Thus, farmers must continually clear new land in order to grow crops.

The Panamanian government passed a land reform law in the 1950s that required land owners to make profitable use of their forested land or be forced to give up that land. As a result, forests—and squirrel monkey habitat—were destroyed to create money–making farms.

The monkeys have also faced the threat of capture. Up through the 1970s, they were taken from their forest habitat and exported around the world for use as pets and in medical research. International treaties now ban the sale and trade of the animals.

Central American squirrel monkeys are protected in the Corcovado National Biological Reserve in southern Costa Rica.

MONKEY, WOOLLY SPIDER
Brachyteles arachnoides

PHYLUM: Chordata
CLASS: Mammalia
ORDER: Primates
FAMILY: Cebidae
STATUS: Endangered, IUCN
Endangered, ESA
RANGE: Brazil

Monkey, woolly spider

Brachyteles arachnoides

Description and biology

The woolly spider monkey, or muriqui, is the largest species of New World (Western Hemisphere) monkey. It has an average head and body length of 18 to 25 inches (46 to 64 centimeters) and weighs between 26 and 33 pounds (12 and 15 kilograms). Its prehensile (able to grasp or hold something by wrapping around it) tail is longer than its body, measuring 25 to 32 inches (64 to 81 centimeters) long. The animal's head is round and small in relation to its body. Its limbs are long. The fur on its body is thick and gold in color. The fur on its face, arms, and legs is black, although sometimes it may be pink or mottled (spotted or streaked).

The woolly spider monkey lives in the crown of the tallest trees and has never been seen on the ground. It moves through

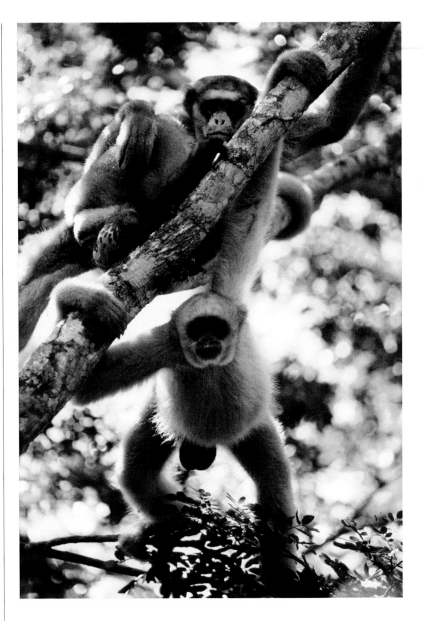

the trees by swinging from branch to branch with its arms. It feeds during the day on leaves, seeds, fruits, and insects.

Most woolly spider monkeys form social groups of 2 to 4 members, although groups of up to 20 or more have been observed in the wild. Mating between males and females may take place at any time. After a gestation (pregnancy) period of four to five months, a female woolly spider monkey gives birth to a single infant.

Habitat and current distribution

The woolly spider monkey prefers to inhabit undisturbed tropical and rain forests. Its range extends only over the southeastern Brazilian states of São Paulo, Espírito Santo, Rio de Janeiro, and Minas Gerais. Biologists (people who study living organisms) estimate that 200 to 400 of the animals currently exist in the wild.

History and conservation measures

The woolly spider monkey once ranged over all Atlantic coastal forests of eastern and southeastern Brazil. It is estimated that the monkey's population in the sixteenth century numbered almost 500,000. By 1972, that population had dropped to 2,000. Today, the animal is almost extinct.

Since the 1800s, the human population in this region of Brazil has swelled enormously. To feed the growing numbers of people, large tracts of forest have been cleared over the years to provide pasture land for cattle and to create coffee, sugar cane, and cocoa plantations. Logging of these forest areas for their valuable timber has also taken its toll. Only two percent of the original forest cover remains in this region.

In the past, woolly spider monkeys were hunted for food. Although currently protected by law, many may still be taken by hunters in some areas.

Small, isolated groups of the animals exist in protected areas. In the state of Minas Gerais, about 50 monkeys live on a private coffee plantation called Fazenda Montes Claros. Another group lives on Fazenda Barreiro Rico, a private ranch in São Paulo. Woolly spider monkeys may also be found in the Biological Reserve of Nova Lombardi in Espírito Santo and in other state and national parks in the region.

NUMBAT
Myrmecobius fasciatus

PHYLUM: Chordata
CLASS: Mammalia
ORDER: Marsupialia
FAMILY: Myrmecobiidae
STATUS: Vulnerable, IUCN
Endangered, ESA
RANGE: Australia

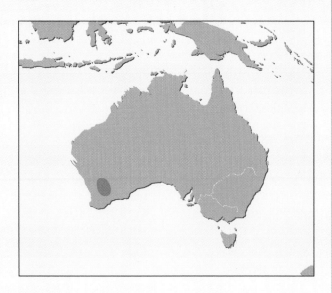

Numbat
Myrmecobius fasciatus

Description and biology

The numbat, also known as the banded anteater, is a very unusual Australian marsupial. Marsupials are an order of mammals whose young continue to develop after birth in a pouch on the outside of the mother's body. Most marsupials are nocturnal (active at night). The numbat, however, does not have a true pouch in which its young develop and it is diurnal (pronounced die–ER–nal; active during the day).

Resembling a squirrel in size, an average numbat has a head and body length of 9 inches (23 centimeters) and a tail length of 7 inches (18 centimeters). It weighs between 14 and 21 ounces (397 and 595 grams). The numbat's coat is reddish brown with white flecks. A series of white stripes stretches across its back all the way to its bushy tail. A dark stripe runs across the animal's eye from its ear to its long, flattened snout.

The numbat feeds chiefly on termites. It uses its sharp–clawed forefeet to dig into termite colonies it finds in

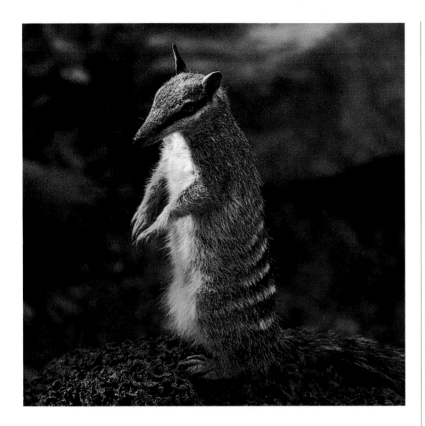

fallen branches. It then uses its long, sticky tongue to remove the termites, which it swallows whole. The animal has a home range of 50 to 120 acres (20 to 48 hectares). At night, it builds a sheltering nest of leaves, grass, and bark in hollow logs or in burrows it digs for itself.

The normally solitary male and female numbat come together only to mate. A female numbat gives birth to four young, usually in January or February. Since she does not have a pouch, her young attach themselves to her nipples and cling to the surrounding hair. They stay attached for six months. Afterward, the female places her young in various nests she has built, moving them between those nests by carrying them on her back. The young numbats eventually leave their mother's home range by November or December.

Habitat and current distribution

Numbats prefer to live in forests dominated by eucalyptus trees that are prone to attack by termites. The animals are currently found only in southwestern Western Australia. Biologists (people who study living organisms) estimate that less than 2,000 numbats exist in the wild.

History and conservation measures

The numbat once ranged throughout southern Australia. Slowly it began to disappear from eastern areas until, by the 1960s, it was found only in the southwestern region of the country. The numbat population continued to decline until 1980, when the Australian government realized that red foxes that had been introduced into numbat habitat were preying on the animals. Since then, the government has controlled the number of foxes in the region and the numbat population has recovered slightly. The Australian government is also trying to relocate numbats to their former eastern habitats.

ORANGUTAN
Pongo pygmaeus

PHYLUM: Chordata
CLASS: Mammalia
ORDER: Primates
FAMILY: Hominidae
STATUS: Vulnerable, IUCN
Endangered, ESA
RANGE: Brunei, Indonesia,
Malaysia

Orangutan
Pongo pygmaeus

Description and biology

The only great ape found in Asia, the orangutan is the largest living arboreal (tree–dwelling) ape. In the Malay language, its name means "forest person" or "man of the woods." With its long, powerful arms and hands and feet that can grasp branches, the animal moves easily from tree to tree. The orangutan's reddish brown coat is long and soft. It has small ears, a bulging snout, and a high forehead. An average orangutan has a head and body length of 30 to 40 inches (76 to 102 centimeters) and a shoulder height of 45 to 60 inches (114 to 152 centimeters). It weighs between 85 and 220 pounds (39 and 100 kilograms). Males are much larger and heavier than females.

Orangutans spend 95 percent of their lives in trees. During the day, the animals feed primarily on fruit. They also eat leaves, insects, bark, and young birds and squirrels. Each night, they build a nest in a tree 35 to 80 feet (11 to 24 meters) above

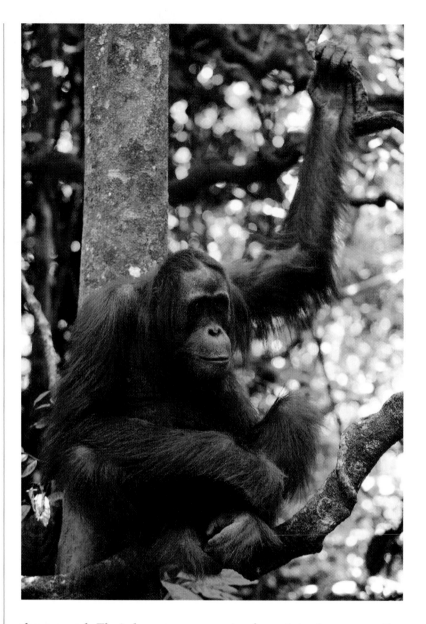

the ground. Their home range varies from 1 to 4 square miles (2.5 to 10 square kilometers).

The orangutan is a solitary animal. The only bond formed is between a mother and her infant. Mating, which can occur at any time during the year, is the only time males and females interact. They stay together for a few days to a few months until the female is pregnant, then they split up. After a gestation (pregnancy) period of 233 to 270 days, a female gives birth to one young. She raises the infant alone, keeping it constantly with her for the first year. She nurses the infant for up to three years. During a normal life span of 40 years, a female will bear only 4 or 5 offspring.

Habitat and current distribution

The orangutan inhabits a variety of forest habitats, including swampy coastal forests, mangrove forests, and mountain forests. It is found only on the Southeast Asian islands of Sumatra (part of the country of Indonesia) and Borneo (divided among Malaysia, Indonesia, and Brunei). In the mid–1990s, biologists (people who study living organisms) estimated that 12,000 to 20,000 orangutans existed on Borneo, while another 9,000 lived on Sumatra.

History and conservation measures

For thousands of years, the orangutan has been a victim of human abuse. Early humans considered it a food source and hunted it to the point of extinction in many areas. Orangutans once ranged throughout Southeast Asia. They now live on only 2 percent of that original range.

The greatest threat to orangutans is habitat destruction. The relentless clearing of rain forests to create plantations on the islands has reduced their habitat by 90 percent in the last 50 years. The animals are driven into forest areas that are too small to support them. Seeking food, the orangutans often wander onto nearby plantations. They are then killed or injured by workers protecting the crops.

In late 1997, orangutans and other wildlife in Southeast Asia suffered terribly from devastating wildfires and smoke that swept across the region. The fires resulted from man–made and natural causes. Farmers in the region rely on slash–and–burn agriculture, a process whereby a forest is cut down and all trees and vegetation are burned to create cleared land. When the El Niño weather pattern delayed the seasonal monsoon rains, hot and dry conditions fanned the fires. Many orangutans died in the fires or from smoke inhalation. Others were killed by frightened villagers as they escaped the burning forests.

Another major threat to orangutans is capture. Thousands of females have been slaughtered so their offspring could be captured and sold as pets. Some childless couples even raise the animals as children, dressing them in human clothes. In the late 1980s and early 1990s, the demand for orangutan pets was especially strong in Taiwan, where a children's television show featured a pet orangutan. Of those infants that are captured in the wild, up to 50 percent die during transport.

Several protected reserves have been established in the orangutan's range, including the Gunung Lueser National Park in northern Sumatra and the Tanjung Puting National Park in Borneo. Conservationists and wildlife researchers have also established camps to help train orangutans that were once pets to return to their natural habitat. However, most of these orangutans have spent too much time among humans and cannot exist in the wild.

ORYX, SCIMITAR–HORNED
Oryx dammah

PHYLUM: Chordata

CLASS: Mammalia

ORDER: Artiodactyla

FAMILY: Bovidae

STATUS: Critically endangered, IUCN

RANGE: Algeria, Burkina Faso, Chad, Egypt, Israel, Libya, Mali, Mauritania, Morocco, Niger, Senegal, Sudan, Tunisia, Western Sahara

Oryx, scimitar–horned
Oryx dammah

Description and biology

The scimitar–horned oryx is a small, horselike antelope. It is so–named because its two horns, which extend back from its head in a long sweeping arc, are similar in shape to scimitars, which are curved, single–edged Asian swords. Most of its body is nearly white in color. Its neck and small portions of its face are dark brown. This oryx has short, rounded ears, large hooves, and a tuft of hair below its chin and at the end of its tail. It also has a short mane extending from its head over its shoulders.

An average scimitar–horned oryx has a head and body length of 60 to 90 inches (152 to 229 centimeters) and weighs 250 to 460 pounds (114 to 209 kilograms). Its tail measures 18 to 35 inches (46 to 89 centimeters) long, while its horns extend 30 to 55 inches (76 to 140 centimeters).

A scimitar–horned oryx with its horns that resemble scimitars, a type of Asian sword.

Scimitar–horned oryx often gather in herds of 20 to 40 members. During the day, the herds travel over great distances to feed on grass and other desert vegetation. The animals are often preyed upon by hyenas and large cats.

Mating may take place between males and females at any time, but births seem to peak during early spring and early fall. Female scimitar–horned oryx give birth to a single infant after a gestation (pregnancy) period of 220 to 253 days.

Habitat and current distribution

Scimitar–horned oryx inhabit the rolling dunes and grassy plains of the desert regions in northern Africa. The greatest population of these oryx, numbering only a few hundred, is found in Chad.

History and conservation measures

This species was once quite common in the areas surrounding the Sahara Desert. Herds sometimes joined together to form groups that numbered in the thousands. In the past few decades, however, desertification, drought, competition from domestic livestock, and uncontrolled hunting by humans have all combined to eliminate this oryx from much of its original habitat.

Desertification is the gradual transformation of productive land into that with desertlike conditions. Even a desert can become desertified, losing its sparse collection of plants and animals and becoming a barren wasteland. Much of the scimitar–horned oryx's habitat has been desertified by natural and man–made actions. Droughts have plagued the region, and overgrazing by farm animals has depleted what little vegetation has been able to grow.

The greatest threat to the scimitar–horned oryx, however, has been hunting. Wanton (merciless) killing by humans has brought the animal to near extinction in several parts of its range during various times of the twentieth century. By the mid–1970s, almost all of the region's scimitar–horned oryx were confined to a single place: the Ouadi Rime–Ouadi Achim Faunal Reserve in Chad. Established in 1969, the reserve was a suitable, well–protected habitat area. By 1978, the oryx population in the reserve numbered about 5,000. That same year, civil war broke out in the country and protection for the reserve ceased. Since then, herds have been scattered throughout unprotected areas and the number of scimitar–horned oryx has decreased greatly.

Otter, marine
Lutra felina

Description and biology

Otters are members of the weasel family. The marine otter, sometimes called the sea cat, has a long body, a flat head, small ears, and a broad, whiskered muzzle. Its short legs and webbed feet help make it an agile swimmer. Thick, glossy dark brown hair covers its body. An average marine otter has a head and body length of 22 to 31 inches (59 to 79 centimeters) and a tail length of 12 to 14 inches (30 to 36 inches). It weighs 7 to 31 pounds (3 to 14 kilograms).

Marine otters feed mainly on crustaceans (such as crabs and shrimp) and mollusk (such as snails, clams, and oysters). While swimming on their backs, they often lay their prey on their chests and use rocks to smash open the hard shells. The otter's main predator is the orca (killer whale).

The otters are primarily solitary animals, but groups of three or more have been observed in the wild. Male and female marine otters mate at any time during the year, although primarily during the summer. After a gestation (pregnancy) period that lasts between 60 and 120 days, female marine otters usually give birth to a litter of two pups.

Habitat and current distribution

The marine otter ranges along the Pacific coastline of Peru and Chile south to the Strait of Magellan, a narrow channel separating South America from Tierra del Fuego and other islands south of the continent. The otters are found primarily in the southern region of their range. One scientific study estimated that the total marine otter population numbers less than 1,000.

Marine otters prefer to inhabit exposed rocky coastal areas and secluded bays and inlets near estuaries (regions where a river empties into an ocean). While searching for freshwater shrimp, marine otters have been known to swim 2,000 feet (610 meters) up a river from the ocean.

History and conservation measures

Marine otters were once plentiful throughout their entire range. However, because the animals have been long hunted for their fur, they are now endangered or on the verge of extinction in many areas. Water pollution also may be responsible for the destruction of sections of their habitat.

International treaties have banned the sale of marine otter pelts, but no other current conservation measures are underway.

PANDA, GIANT
Ailuropoda melanoleuca

PHYLUM: Chordata
CLASS: Mammalia
ORDER: Carnivora
FAMILY: Ursidae
STATUS: Endangered, IUCN
Endangered, ESA
RANGE: China

Panda, giant
Ailuropoda melanoleuca

Description and biology

Recognized worldwide, the giant panda has become a symbol in the fight to save endangered species from extinction. The animal shares many characteristics with both bears and raccoons. Since recent genetic tests reveal it is more closely related to the bear, scientists classify it as a member of the bear family (Ursidae).

An average giant panda has a head and body length of 4 to 6 feet (1.2 to 1.8 meters) and weighs between 165 and 350 pounds (75 and 160 kilograms). Its tail measures 5 inches (13 centimeters) in length. The animal's thick, woolly coat is primarily white. Its legs, shoulders, ears, and eye patches are black.

A giant panda eating. These animals spend 10 to 16 hours a day consuming food.

134

Bamboo stalks and roots make up 95 percent of the giant panda's diet. One of its wrist bones is enlarged and elongated, and the animal uses it like a thumb when grasping stalks of bamboo. The giant panda also has strong jaws and teeth to crush bamboo. The remainder of its diet is made up of grass, bulbs, insects, rodents, and fish. The animal spends 10 to 16 hours eating the 20 to 40 pounds (9 to 18 kilograms) of food it needs each day.

Giant pandas are solitary and territorial. They have a home range of 1.5 to 2.5 square miles (4 to 6.5 square kilometers), which they mark with secretions from scent glands. Males and females come together to mate between March and May. After a gestation (pregnancy) period of 125 to 150 days, a female giant panda gives birth to one to two cubs in a sheltered den. The cubs are very fragile at birth, weighing only 3 to 5 ounces (85 to 142 grams). If two cubs are born, usually just one survives. It remains with its mother for up to a year. The average life span of a giant panda in the wild is 15 years.

Habitat and current distribution

Among the rarest mammals in the world, giant pandas are found only in the mountains of central China, in the Sichuan, Shaanxi, and Gansu provinces. Biologists (people who study living organisms) estimate that about 1,000 giant pandas exist in the wild. The animals prefer to inhabit dense bamboo and coniferous (cone bearing) forests at elevations between 5,000 and 10,000 feet (1,525 and 3,050 meters).

History and conservation measures

The giant panda has existed in China for hundreds of thousands of years. It was once common throughout the country, but over the last 2,000 years it has disappeared from Henan, Hubei, Hunan, Guizhou, and Yunnan provinces. In 1869, the French missionary and naturalist Armand David became the first European to describe the giant panda. The species was not well known in the West until a captive specimen was brought to the United States in the 1930s. As a gesture of goodwill, the Chinese government presented U.S. president Richard Nixon with a pair of giant pandas (Ling–Ling and Hsing–Hsing) in 1972. The animals were kept at the National Zoo in Washington, D.C.

Habitat destruction is the primary danger to giant pandas. Since bamboo grows slowly, the pandas need a large range in which to feed. This range is constantly being threatened by China's growing human population—estimated at over 1,000,000,000. To help save the dwindling giant panda population, the Chinese government has set aside 11 nature preserves where bamboo flourishes.

Another threat to the giant panda is poaching, or illegal killing. The animal is protected by international treaties, and the Chinese government sentences those convicted of poaching a giant panda to life in prison. Nonetheless, the animal is still hunted for its fur, which is sold illegally in Southeast Asian markets at a high price.

More than 100 giant pandas are currently found in Chinese zoos. Several others are housed in North Korean zoos. Only about 15 giant pandas live in zoos outside of these two countries. The animals are often difficult to breed in captivity. The first giant panda birth outside China occurred at the Mexico City Zoo in 1980.

PANDA, RED
Ailurus fulgens

PHYLUM: Chordata
CLASS: Mammalia
ORDER: Carnivora
FAMILY: Procyonidae
STATUS: Endangered, IUCN
RANGE: Bhutan, China, India, Laos, Myanmar, Nepal

Panda, red
Ailurus fulgens

Description and biology

The red panda, also known as the lesser panda, has rust–colored fur with chocolate brown markings. The Chinese call this striking animal "firefox" because of its flame–colored fur. The red panda has short, pointed ears and a mask similar to a raccoon's. In fact, the red panda is considered a member of the raccoon family, unlike its relative the giant panda, which is a member of the bear family.

An average red panda has a head and body length of 20 to 23.5 inches (51 to 60 centimeters) and weighs between 7.7 and 11 pounds (3.5 and 5 kilograms). Its banded tail measures 12 to 20 inches (30 to 51 centimeters) in length. The animal is most active at dawn and at dusk. Although it spends most of its time in trees, it feeds on the ground. Its diet consists mainly of bamboo leaves, but it also eats grasses, berries, fruits, roots, and other plant matter.

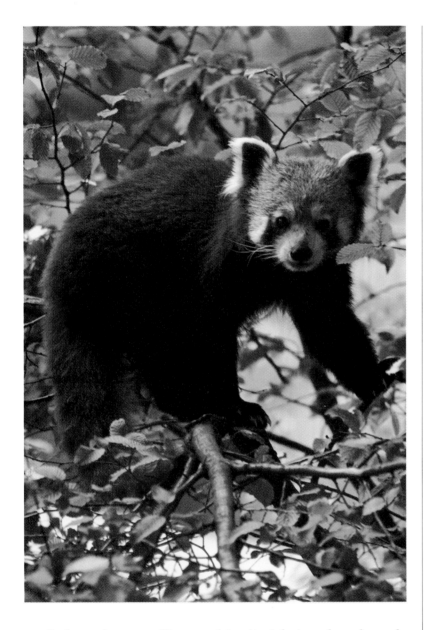

A red panda perched in a tree. The animal is sometimes called the "firefox" by the Chinese because of its flame–colored fur.

Red pandas are solitary and territorial. A male red panda will often patrol the boundary of his territory, while a female will often remain in the center of hers. The territory of a single male will overlap the territories of several females. Males and females come together to mate in January and February. During the courtship period, males and females will groom each other. After mating is complete, the male leaves and will not care for the female or her young. A female red panda gives birth to 1 to 4 cubs in a secure den (hollow tree, cave, or rock crevice) after a gestation (pregnancy) period of 90 to 145 days. The newborn pandas are tan in color, blind, and totally dependent on their mother. They nurse for about 5 months, then begin eating bamboo leaves. A month later, they leave to stake out their own territories.

Habitat and current distribution

The red panda is found in the Himalayas and other mountains in northern India, southern China, Nepal, Bhutan, northern Myanmar, and northern Laos. It inhabits mountain spruce and fir forests at elevations between 6,500 and 13,000 feet (1,980 and 3,960 meters). The animal has been studied extensively only in Nepal. Scientists are unsure of the total number of red pandas in existence.

History and conservation measures

The major threat to red pandas is the loss of their habitat. Forests throughout much of the animal's range have been cleared to create farmland to feed a growing human population. In areas where forests have not been completely cleared, many trees have been cut down for use as fuel or building materials. The little "islands" of forest that remain are often not large enough to support the number of red pandas that have been forced to live there. With limited food sources, many of the animals starve to death.

Because of its attractive fur, the red panda has been hunted for its coat. Traps set for other animals in its range, such as the musk deer, also have taken their toll on the red panda. International treaties prohibit the trading of red panda pelts, and the animal is fully protected in China and Nepal.

In China, a number of red pandas also benefit by inhabiting the parks and reserves that have been set up for giant pandas. Displayed in zoos worldwide, red pandas have been bred in captivity with reasonable success. The International Red Panda Management Group is leading an effort to unite breeding programs around the world into a single global program.

PORCUPINE, THIN–SPINED
Chaetomys subspinosus

PHYLUM: Chordata
CLASS: Mammalia
ORDER: Rodentia
FAMILY: Echimyidae
STATUS: Vulnerable, IUCN
Endangered, ESA
RANGE: Brazil

Porcupine, thin–spined

Chaetomys subspinosus

Description and biology

The thin–spined porcupine, also known as the bristle–spined porcupine, gets its common names from the thin, bristly spines that cover its body. The animal is not considered a member of the family of true porcupines, but a member of the family of spiny rats. Unlike true porcupines, the thin–spined porcupine has no spines on its lower back. The spines on the animal's head and shoulders are kinky and short, just 0.6 inch (1.5 centimeters) in length. Those on its upper back, legs, and tail are wavier and longer, up to 2 inches (5 centimeters) in length. The spines are usually tricolored, ranging from pale yellow at the base to dark brown in the middle and back to pale yellow at the tip. The animal's body is brownish gray in color, while its feet and tail are darker.

An average thin–spined porcupine has a head and body length of 15 to 18 inches (38 to 46 centimeters) and a tail length of 10 inches (25 centimeters). All four of the animal's limbs have four digits (resembling human fingers or toes), which end in long, curved claws. These sharp claws help make the thin–spined porcupine an excellent climber, able to scale stone walls.

The thin–spined porcupine is nocturnal (active at night), feeding on fruits and cocoa tree nuts. Biologists (people who study living organisms) have been unable to study the animal well enough to learn its social structure or its reproductive habits.

Habitat and current distribution

The thin–spined porcupine is found only in the eastern and southeastern Brazilian states of Bahia, Sergipe, Espírito Santo, and Rio de Janeiro. It inhabits the edges of Atlantic coastal forests near open areas. The number of thin–spined porcupine existing in the wild is unknown, but the animal is believed to be quite rare.

History and conservation measures

The main threat facing the thin–spined porcupine is the loss of its habitat due to forest clear–cutting (process of cutting down all the trees in a forest area). Because scientists and conservationists (people protecting the natural world) know very little about the habits of the animal, saving its forest ecosystem (animals, plants, and microorganisms with their environment) is the best strategy to preserve the thin–spined porcupine. Other highly endangered species that inhabit the same ecosystem, such as the golden lion tamarin and the woolly spider monkey, would be saved at the same time.

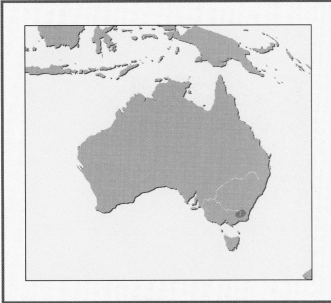

POSSUM, MOUNTAIN PYGMY
Burramys parvus

PHYLUM: Chordata

CLASS: Mammalia

ORDER: Marsupialia

FAMILY: Burramyidae

STATUS: Endangered, IUCN
Endangered, ESA

RANGE: Australia

Possum, mountain pygmy

Burramys parvus

Description and biology

The mountain pygmy possum is a small marsupial (mammal whose young continue to develop after birth in a pouch on the outside of the mother's body). It has an average head and body length of 4 to 5 inches (10 to 13 centimeters) and weight of just 1 to 2 ounces (28 to 57 grams). Its 5.5–inch (14–centimeter) tail is prehensile, meaning it can hold onto items such as tree limbs by wrapping around them. The animal is covered with brownish gray fur that ends at the base of its tail.

Nocturnal (active during the night), the mountain pygmy possum forages on the ground and in trees for seeds, fruit, leaves, and insects. It is the only marsupial that stores seeds for use during the winter.

Male and female mountain pygmy possums mate in late October and early November. After a gestation (pregnancy) period of only 13 to 16 days, a female mountain pygmy pos-

Although preyed on by foxes and cats, the mountain pygmy possum's main threat is destruction of its Australian habitat.

sum gives birth to a litter of four. The young remain in the mother's pouch for at least three weeks and are nursed for up to nine weeks.

Habitat and current distribution

Mountain pygmy possums inhabit the mountains of eastern Victoria and southeastern New South Wales in Australia. The animals are most often found at elevations between 5,000 and 6,000 feet (1,525 and 1,830 meters), living among the loose stones or rocky debris at the base of a slope or cliff. Biologists (people who study living organisms) believe around 900 of these animals exist in the wild.

History and conservation measures

Before the mid–1960s, the mountain pygmy possum was known only from fossilized remains found in New South

Wales. A live mountain pygmy possum was then found and identified in Victoria. Further animals were later found in New South Wales.

The main threat to the mountain pygmy possum is habitat destruction caused by the development of ski resorts. It is also preyed upon by cats and foxes.

Mountain pygmy possums are protected in the Bogong National Park in Victoria and the Mount Kosciusko National Park in New South Wales.

PRAIRIE DOG, MEXICAN
Cynomys mexicanus

PHYLUM: Chordata
CLASS: Mammalia
ORDER: Rodentia
FAMILY: Sciuridae
STATUS: Endangered, IUCN
Endangered, ESA
RANGE: Mexico

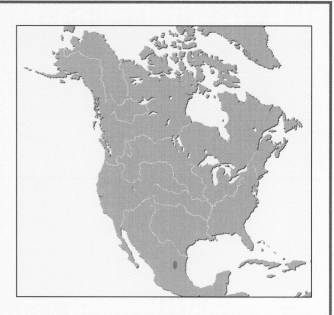

Prairie dog, Mexican

Cynomys mexicanus

Description and biology

The Mexican prairie dog is a large, stout member of the squirrel family, closely related to ground squirrels, chipmunks, and marmots. An average Mexican prairie dog measures 12 to 16 inches (30 to 41 centimeters) in length and weighs 1.5 to 3 pounds (0.7 to 1.4 kilograms). The animal's buff–colored fur is tinted with black, white, red, and yellow. The tip of its short tail is black. Twice a year, its fur is shed and replaced by a new coat (a process called molting).

Like other prairie dogs, the Mexican prairie dog is active above ground during the day. It feeds on grasses and other plants. Badgers, coyotes, weasels, eagles, hawks, and snakes are its main predators.

Mexican prairie dogs live in coteries, or groups, in large burrows they have dug with several entrances. A coterie is made up of one or two adult males, one to four adult females, and a number of young. Mating between males and females usually takes place between late January and July. After a gestation (pregnancy) period of about 30 days, a female Mexican prairie dog gives birth to a varying number of pups.

Habitat and current distribution

The Mexican prairie dog is found only in northeastern Mexico in the states of Coahuila and San Luis Potosi. The animal prefers to inhabit open plains, valleys, and plateaus at elevations between 5,200 and 7,200 feet (1,600 and 2,200 meters). Biologists (people who study living organisms) do not know the total number of Mexican prairie dogs currently in existence.

History and conservation measures

The greatest threat to the Mexican prairie dog is habitat loss. Much of its former habitat has been destroyed to create farmland to feed a growing human population. Some colonies of Mexican prairie dogs have been intentionally poisoned by humans who view the animals as pests that destroy crops and grazing land.

Since little is known about the Mexican prairie dog's habits and biology, no specific conservation measures have been devised.

RABBIT, VOLCANO
Romerolagus diazi

PHYLUM: Chordata
CLASS: Mammalia
ORDER: Lagomorpha
FAMILY: Leporidae
STATUS: Endangered, IUCN
Endangered, ESA
RANGE: Mexico

Rabbit, volcano
Romerolagus diazi

Description and biology

The volcano rabbit, also known as the Mexican pygmy rabbit, has short, thick dark brown hair. It is one of the few species of short–eared rabbits. Its rounded ears measure just 1.6 inches (4 centimeters) long. The animal also has short hind legs and feet and a very short tail. An average volcano rabbit has a head and body length of 10.5 to 13 inches (26.5 to 33 centimeters) and weighs between 14 and 18 ounces (397 and 510 grams).

Active mainly during the day, the volcano rabbit feeds on the tender young leaves of zacaton or bunchgrass (various wiry grass species that grow in low clumps in Mexico and the southwestern United States). Its main predators are long–tailed weasels, bobcats, and rattlesnakes.

A volcano rabbit blending in with its surroundings.

Volcano rabbits construct elaborate burrows in deep sandy soil. Entrances are hidden in the base of grass clumps. For temporary shelter during the day, the animals sometimes use abandoned pocket–gopher burrows or the hollows between rocks and boulders.

Scientists know little about the social structure of volcano rabbits. Groups of two to seven animals have been observed in the wild. Male and female volcano rabbits mate primarily between January and April. After a gestation (pregnancy) period of 38 to 40 days, a female gives birth to a litter of one to five infants.

Habitat and current distribution

The volcano rabbit is found only in central Mexico on the slopes of four volcanoes: Popocatépetl, Iztaccíhautl, El Pelado, and Tláloc. The animal inhabits pine forests on those slopes at elevations between 9,000 and 14,000 feet (2,740 and 4,270 meters). These areas are often dry in the winter and rainy in the summer. Biologists (people who study living organisms) are unsure of the total number of volcano rabbits currently in existence.

History and conservation measures

The volcano rabbit has traditionally been hunted for food and sport. Although laws have been passed outlawing the hunting of the animals, they are seldom enforced.

Forest fires, the conversion of forest land into farmland, the overgrazing of cattle and sheep, and the cutting of trees for timber have all contributed to the destruction of volcano rabbit habitat. Many of the forest fires result when farmers burn bunchgrass areas in hopes of promoting new growth for their livestock (a process known as slash–and–burn agriculture).

Each of the remaining volcano rabbit populations lies within a 45–minute drive of Mexico City. Now the world's largest city, it has a rapidly growing population of 20,000,000 people. As the city and rural settlements around it continue to expand, volcano rabbit habitat continues to decrease. As of 1998, only 16 patches of suitable habitat exist.

Part of the volcano rabbit's present–day range lies within the Izta–Popo and Zoquiapan National Parks. However, habitat destruction continues even with these protected areas.

RHINOCEROS, BLACK
Diceros bicornis

PHYLUM: Chordata
CLASS: Mammalia
ORDER: Perissodactyla
FAMILY: Rhinocerotidae
STATUS: Critically endangered, IUCN
Endangered, ESA
RANGE: Angola, Botswana, Cameroon, Ethiopia, Kenya, Malawi, Mozambique, Namibia, Rwanda, South Africa, Swaziland, Tanzania, Zambia, Zimbabwe

Rhinoceros, black

Diceros bicornis

Description and biology

The black rhinoceros is one of two species of rhinoceros found in Africa (the other is the white rhinoceros). Despite its name, the animal is actually gray in color. An average black rhinoceros has a head and body length of 9 to 12 feet (2.7 to 3.7 meters), stands 4.5 to 5.25 feet (1.4 to 1.6 meters) tall at its shoulder, and weighs between 2,000 and 4,000 pounds (908 and 1,816 kilograms). The animal's huge size is deceiving, as it can move quite quickly when it decides to charge. It has very poor eyesight—it can see clearly only up to 30 feet (9 meters) away—but acute senses of hearing and smell.

Rhinoceros means "horn nosed." The black rhinoceros has two horns on its snout. The front one is longer and can measure up to 53 inches (135 centimeters). The animal uses its horns (made of keratin fibers, the same substance as in hu-

151

Although named the black rhinoceros, the animal is often gray in color.

man fingernails) to dig in the ground for mineral salt, to defend its territory against other rhinos, and to defend itself against predators such as lions and hyenas.

The black rhinoceros protects itself against the intense African heat by sleeping during the day in a patch of brush. It awakens in the cool of the evening to begin feeding. The animal is an herbivore (plant–eater), eating branches, leaves, and bark. Its pointed upper lip is prehensile, meaning the lip can actually grasp branches to help pull and break them.

Black rhinos are mostly solitary animals, and males and females come together only to mate. Mating may take place at any time during the year. Males will often fight over the right to mate with a female, and males and females often fight during their courtship. After a gestation (pregnancy) period of 15 to 18 months, a female black rhinoceros gives birth to a single calf, which weighs about 90 pounds (41 kilograms). The calf nurses for up to two years and remains dependent on its mother for another year. Black rhinos have an average life span of 30 to 35 years.

Habitat and current distribution

The black rhinoceros is found only in small pockets in eastern and southern Africa. Its total population is estimated between 2,000 and 3,000. The animal prefers to inhabit open dry scrublands, savannas, dense thickets, and mountain forests.

History and conservation measures

The black rhinoceros is disappearing faster than any large animal on the planet. It once ranged widely throughout the savannas of Africa. In 1970, biologists (people who study living organisms) estimated that the black rhinoceros population numbered 65,000. By the late 1990s, that number had dropped by over 95 percent. At that rate, black rhinos may be extinct by the early twenty–first century.

The direct cause for the decline of black rhinos is the demand for their horns. For centuries, people in Asia have believed that the powder of ground rhino horns can cure fevers, nose bleeds, measles, food poisoning, and other illnesses. Many believe it increases sexual desire and stamina, as well. Rhino horns have also been used to make handles for the traditional "jambia" daggers worn by men in Yemen.

International treaties now outlaw the trade or sale of any rhino products. Nonetheless, poaching continues. A pound of rhino horn powder can sell for as much as $2,000. The animal's skin, blood, and urine are also sold. In the late 1980s, some wildlife agencies in Africa began tranquilizing black rhinos and removing their horns so the animals would not be as attractive to poachers. These attempts have proved fruitless, as over 100 dehorned black rhinos have since been slaughtered by poachers.

In 1994, the U.S. Congress passed the Rhino and Tiger Conservation Act. This measure provides financial assistance for the development of conservation measures for rhinos and tigers.

RHINOCEROS, NORTHERN WHITE

Ceratotherium simum cottoni

PHYLUM: Chordata
CLASS: Mammalia
ORDER: Perissodactyla
FAMILY: Rhinocerotidae
STATUS: Critically endangered, IUCN
Endangered, ESA
RANGE: Congo, Sudan

Rhinoceros, northern white

Ceratotherium simum cottoni

Description and biology

The northern white rhinoceros is also called the northern square–lipped rhinoceros. The animal derives its common name from the Afrikaans (language of white South Africans of Dutch descent) word *weit,* meaning "wide." The reference is to the animal's wide snout. However, the word *weit* was mistranslated as "white," and so the animal is now known as the white rhinoceros.

The white rhinoceros is not actually white but light gray in color. Two subspecies of white rhinoceroses exist in Africa: the southern white rhinoceros and the northern white rhinoceros. The southern white rhinoceros is found in South Africa, Swaziland, Namibia, Botswana, Zimbabwe, Mozambique, Zambia, and Kenya. The most common of all rhinos, its population numbers about 7,500.

The northern white rhinoceros has a large, square–shaped mouth that allows it to graze on short grass. The second largest land mammal (only elephants are larger), an average northern white rhinoceros has a head and body length of 12 to 13 feet (3.7 to 4 meters) and stands 5 to 6.5 feet (1.5 to 2 meters) tall at its shoulder. Its tail measures 20 to 28 inches (51 to 71 centimeters) long. The animal may weigh between 5,000 and 8,000 pounds (2,270 and 3,630 kilograms). Despite its large size, the northern white rhinoceros can gallop as fast as 25 miles per hour (40 kilometers per hour).

Northern white rhinoceroses have short legs, broad ears, and two horns on their snout (rhinoceros means "horn–nosed"). White rhinos have the largest horns of any rhino-

Although light–gray in color, a mistranslation of the Afrikaans word weit *has lead to the animal becoming known as the northern white rhinoceros.*

ceros species, measuring 18 to 48 inches (46 to 122 centimeters) in length. They use their horns to fight over territory and females, to defend themselves against predators such as lions and hyenas, and to dig in the ground for mineral salt. The animals have poor vision, but highly developed senses of hearing and smell.

During the heat of the day, northern white rhinoceroses rest in shady spots. To keep cool, they often wallow in mud. When no water is available, they roll in dust to keep cool and to keep insects away. They feed in the evening and in the early morning. Average feeding territory is about 0.75 square miles (2 square kilometers). Females have larger territories than males.

Male and female northern white rhinoceroses come together only to mate. Mating can take place any time of the year, but peaks in February and June. The courtship period may last between 5 and 20 days. After a gestation (pregnancy) period of about 16 months, a female gives birth to a single calf. The mother tends to the calf for two years before chasing it away to live on its own.

Habitat and current distribution

The northern white rhinoceros prefers to inhabit open grasslands and savannas that have water available. Critically endangered, the animal is found only in Congo and southern Sudan in central Africa. Its population is extremely low. Most northern white rhinoceros live in the Garamba National Park in Congo.

History and conservation measures

The northern white rhinoceros is one of the most endangered animals in Africa. In 1980, 821 of the animals existed in the wild. Just six years later, only 17 remained in Congo (then Zaire). Intensive conservation measures were begun and by 1993, the northern white rhinoceros population had increased to 33.

The northern white rhinoceros was driven to the brink of extinction by hunting, specifically for its horns (made of keratin fibers, the same material in human fingernails). For hundreds of years, humans in Asia have used the powder of ground rhino horns in medicines and aphrodisiacs (pronounced af–row–DEEZ–ee–aks; drugs or food that stimulate sexual desire).

In the Middle East, daggers with rhino–horn handles are highly valued.

Despite international treaties currently banning the sale of any rhino products, poaching (illegal hunting) of the animals continues.

RICE RAT, SILVER
Oryzomys palustris natator

PHYLUM: Chordata
CLASS: Mammalia
ORDER: Rodentia
FAMILY: Muridae
STATUS: Endangered, ESA
RANGE: USA (Florida)

Rice rat, silver
Oryzomys palustris natator

Description and biology

The silver rice rat is a small rodent. It has a head and body length of 10 inches (25 centimeters) and a tail length of 5 inches (13 centimeters). The silver–gray color of the coarse fur on its back gives the animal its name.

The nocturnal (active at night) silver rice rat is a good swimmer. It feeds on seeds, insects, small crabs, and the succulent (sap–filled) parts of plants. Predators of the silver rice rat include foxes, skunks, snakes, and raccoons.

Biologists (people who study living organisms) know very little about the animal's breeding behavior, but they believe a female silver rice rat gives birth to one to five young after a gestation (pregnancy) period of about 25 days.

Habitat and current distribution

Found throughout Florida, the silver rice rat is most endangered in the lower Florida Keys in Monroe County. It

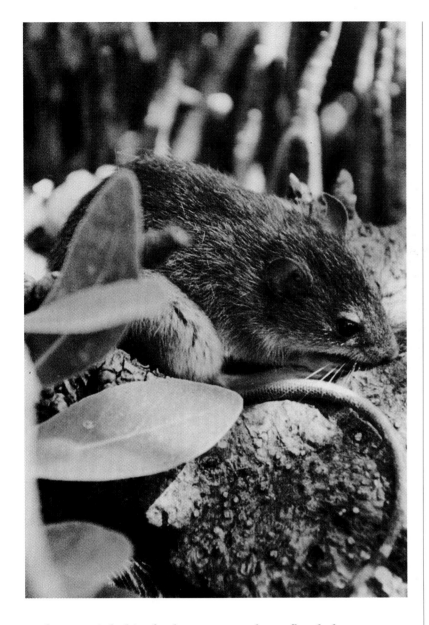

prefers to inhabit freshwater marshes, flooded mangrove swamps, and saltmarsh flats.

History and conservation measures

The silver rice rat faces the threat of habitat destruction as humans continue to develop areas in the Florida Keys. Much of its wetland habitat has been drained to create land suitable for homes and businesses.

Although the silver rice rat is preyed upon by a number of species, its most serious predator is the raccoon, which is native to the Florida Keys. As human development has increased on the islands, so has the amount of garbage. With an increased food source (the garbage), the raccoon population has grown unnaturally high. This has thrown the normal predator–prey relationship between the raccoon and the silver rice rat out of balance, and the number of silver rice rats has declined as a result.

SEAL, GUADALUPE FUR
Arctocephalus townsendi

PHYLUM: Chordata
CLASS: Mammalia
ORDER: Carnivora
FAMILY: Otariidae
STATUS: Vulnerable, IUCN
Threatened, ESA
RANGE: Mexico, USA (California)

Seal, Guadalupe fur

Arctocephalus townsendi

Description and biology

Fur seals and sea lions differ from true seals in that they have external ear flaps. They are also able to turn their hind flippers forward for walking on land. While they use all four flippers for walking, they use only their long front flippers for swimming.

The Guadalupe fur seal can be distinguished from other fur seals by its long, pointed snout and light–colored whiskers. An average male Guadalupe fur seal may grow up to 6.5 feet (2 meters) in length and weigh up to 310 pounds (141 kilograms). Females are smaller, reaching 4.4 feet (1.3 meters) in length and weighing 110 pounds (50 kilograms).

Guadalupe fur seals have a behavioral trait that makes them unique among seals. When on land, they often retreat onto rocky recesses or into caves. Some scientists believe this trait developed in the species in the nineteenth century when hunters mercilessly slaughtered the animals. To survive, Guadalupe fur seals withdrew to caves, a behavior that has since been passed down to the current generation.

The Guadalupe fur seal's diet includes squid and fish such as the lantern fish. The animal travels widely at sea and has been found 186 miles (300 kilometers) away from its main home range. Unlike other seals, the Guadalupe fur seal may be found on shore at any time during the year.

Mating between male and female Guadalupe fur seals takes place between May and July. Males compete with each other over the right to mate with females. A dominant male may breed with as many as ten females. After a gestation (pregnancy) period of about 12 months, a female Guadalupe fur seal gives birth in a cave to one or two pups.

Habitat and current distribution

Guadalupe fur seals range in the Pacific Ocean from the Farallon Islands off the coast of San Francisco, California, south to Islas Revillagigedo, a group of islands 450 miles (724 kilometers) off the coast of the Mexican state of Colima. The animals are known to breed only on the rocky east coast of Guadalupe Island, located west of the Baja California peninsula. Biologists (people who study living organisms) estimate the total Guadalupe fur seal population to be 6,000.

History and conservation measures

As many as 200,000 Guadalupe fur seals may have existed on Guadalupe Island alone before the nineteenth century. Hunters seeking the animals' fur and blubber (fat that was melted down to make oil) nearly wiped out the species. In fact, the Guadalupe fur seal was considered extinct until 1928, when two males were caught by fishermen. In 1954, a small breeding colony of 14 seals was discovered on Guadalupe Island. Since then, the population of Guadalupe fur seals has slowly increased.

In 1922, the Mexican government declared Guadalupe Island a wildlife sanctuary. In 1978, it declared all islands around Baja California wildlife reserves.

Despite these protective measures, the Guadalupe fur seal remains vulnerable because it has little fear of humans. Although legally protected, the animal may still fall prey to hunters. Noise from cruise ships and other human activities often prevents the Guadalupe fur seal from breeding.

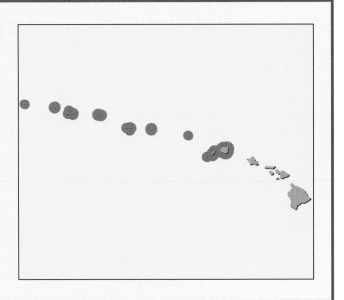

SEAL, HAWAIIAN MONK
Monachus schauinslandi

PHYLUM: Chordata

CLASS: Mammalia

ORDER: Carnivora

FAMILY: Phocidae

STATUS: Endangered, IUCN
Endangered, ESA

RANGE: USA (Hawaii)

Seal, Hawaiian monk
Monachus schauinslandi

Description and biology

The Hawaiian monk seal is a large warm-water seal. It is a member of the family of true seals because it does not have external ear flaps as fur seals and sea lions do. An average Hawaiian monk seal measures 7 to 7.5 feet (2.1 to 2.3 meters) long and weighs 450 to 550 pounds (204 to 250 kilograms). Unlike in most other species, female Hawaiian monk seals are larger than their male counterparts. The color of a monk seal's body varies slightly, from slate gray on top to silver gray underneath.

Hawaiian monk seals eat a variety of aquatic animals, including fish, eels, and octopi. They feed mainly along the shorelines of the islands they inhabit. Sharks often prey upon the seals.

Male Hawaiian monk seals choose a mate by wandering the beaches where females sun themselves. Since there are three times as many males as females, the females are often disturbed. When a male and female decide to mate, they do

A sunning Hawaiian monk seal. In order to survive the seals must have an undisturbed habitat with as little human contact as possible.

so in the water. After a gestation (pregnancy) period of about 330 days, a female Hawaiian monk seal gives birth on the beach to a single pup. She nurses the pup for five weeks, during which time she fasts (does not eat). At birth, the pups are weak swimmers, and they must practice under their mother's supervision until they are weaned.

Habitat and current distribution

The Hawaiian monk seal inhabits the islands and atolls (ring–shaped reefs surrounding lagoons) of the northwestern Hawaiian Islands. Breeding takes place primarily around Nihoa Island, Necker Island, French Frigate Shoals, Laysan Island, Lisianski Island, Pearl and Hermes Reef, the Midway Islands, and Kure Atoll. An estimated 1,200 Hawaiian monk seals remain in the wild.

Although some Hawaiian monk seals move between islands, most remain fairly close to their home beaches.

History and conservation measures

Hawaiian monk seals evolved in an environment totally free of humans. Since they did not know humans, they had no fear of them when contact was made. This made them easy prey for nineteenth–century hunters who sought their fur and blubber (fat that was melted down to make oil). Hunting was so rampant during this period, the species was pushed to the brink of extinction.

The population of Hawaiian monk seals increased slightly, however, in the early twentieth century as the animals sought out undisturbed, remote areas. During World War II (1939–45), humans began occupying more and more of the Hawaiian Islands, and the seals suffered. Any intrusion into their range has a negative effect on the seals. When disturbed by humans, a pregnant female may abort her fetus. If a nursing female is disturbed, she may be unable to continue nursing and her pup may die.

Increased fishing activity in the Hawaiian monk seal's range leads to conflicts between fishermen and seals. Many fishermen kill the seals, believing the animals steal their catch and damage their fishing nets. Some seals do become entangled in fishing nets and drown.

In 1940, a number of the islands and atolls in the Hawaiian monk seal's range were designated the Hawaiian Islands National Wildlife Refuge. In 1976, this area was further declared a Research Natural Area. These protective measures limit the number of human landings on the islands, insuring that Hawaiian monk seals—among the most endangered seals in the world—remain as undisturbed as possible.

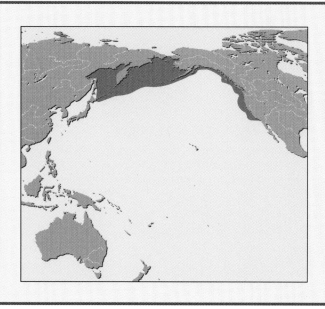

SEA LION, STELLAR'S
Eumetopias jubatus

PHYLUM: Chordata
CLASS: Mammalia
ORDER: Carnivora
FAMILY: Otariidae
STATUS: Endangered, IUCN
Threatened, ESA
RANGE: Canada, Japan, Russia,
USA (Alaska, California, Oregon,
Washington)

Sea lion, Stellar's
Eumetopias jubatus

Description and biology

Sea lions and fur seals are members of the family of eared seals. They differ from true seals in that they have external ear flaps, a flexible neck, and hind flippers that can be turned forward for walking on land.

The Stellar's sea lion, also known as the northern sea lion, is one of the largest species of sea lion. Males may grow up to 13 feet (4 meters) in length and weigh as much as 2,200 pounds (1,000 kilograms). Females are much smaller, weighing about half as much. The sea lion's thin coat of short, coarse hair is tawny brown in color.

Stellar's sea lions feed primarily on fishes, squids, octopi, and crustaceans (shellfish such as shrimp and crabs). They hunt in relatively shallow waters, but can make 20–minute dives down to depths of about 650 feet (198 meters).

During the spring breeding season, the sea lions gather in large groups called rookeries. The Aleutian Islands, a chain of

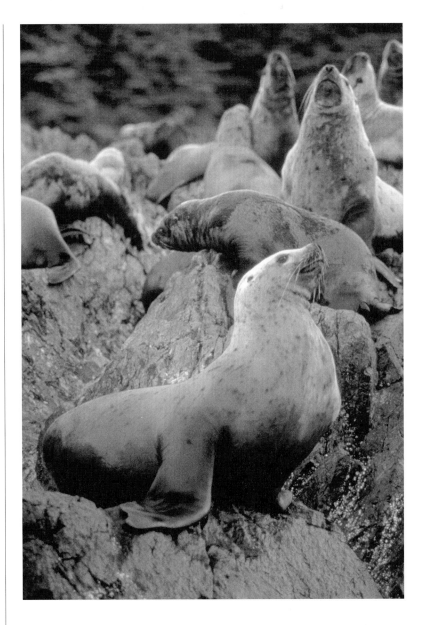

volcanic islands curving in an arc about 1,200 miles (1,931 kilometers) west off the Alaska Peninsula, are one of the animals' principle gathering places. Males come ashore first and stake out their individual territories, occasionally through fighting. They will try to mate with females that pass through their territory. A dominant male who is able to defend his territory successfully may mate with as many as 30 females over a two–month period.

Females arrive on the islands shortly after the males. They first give birth to pups that had been conceived during the previous breeding season. A few weeks later, they are ready to mate again. The pups remain dependent on their mothers for about a year.

Habitat and current distribution

Stellar's sea lions inhabit the coastal waters around rocky islands. They occasionally come on shore to rest and sun themselves on the beaches. Their range extends from the Aleutian Islands west into the Bering Sea and down the Asian coast to northern Japan, and east into the Gulf of Alaska and down the Canadian and American coasts to southern California.

History and conservation measures

Stellar's sea lions, along with other sea lions, were hunted extensively in the nineteenth century for their hides and blubber (fat that was melted down to make oil). In the twentieth century, they have been killed by fishermen who have blamed the animals for robbing their catch of fish.

In 1972, the U.S. Congress passed the Marine Mammal Act, which prohibited the hunting of sea lions in U.S. territorial waters. The Stellar's sea lion received further protection in 1990 when it was placed on the Endangered Species List. The National Marine Fisheries Service has acted to protect breeding spots from shipping and to reduce the number of accidental deaths of sea lions during commercial fishing operations.

Despite these protective measures, the population of Stellar's sea lions continues to decline. Disease, pollution, predators, habitat destruction, and other possible causes have all been investigated. Not one of these has proven conclusive. Scientists remain baffled as to the reason. If the decline continues unchecked, the Stellar's sea lion may soon disappear from most of its range.

TAMARIN, GOLDEN LION
Leontopithecus rosalia

PHYLUM: Chordata
CLASS: Mammalia
ORDER: Primates
FAMILY: Callitrichidae
STATUS: Critically endangered, IUCN
Endangered, ESA
RANGE: Brazil

Tamarin, golden lion
Leontopithecus rosalia

Description and biology

Tamarins, also known as marmosets, are unique New World (Western Hemisphere) monkeys that have a golden mane and long, silky fur. The most striking of the tamarins is the golden lion tamarin, which has a flaming reddish-gold coat and a luxuriant mane. It has an average head and body length of 8 to 13 inches (20 to 33 centimeters) and weighs between 21 and 28 ounces (595 and 794 grams). Its furry tail measures 12 to 16 inches (30 to 41 centimeters) long.

Golden lion tamarins are tree dwellers. Active during the day, they travel from tree to tree, feeding on fruit, insects, plant matter, and other small animals.

The animals often form family groups ranging from two to eight members. A male–female pair forms the center of the

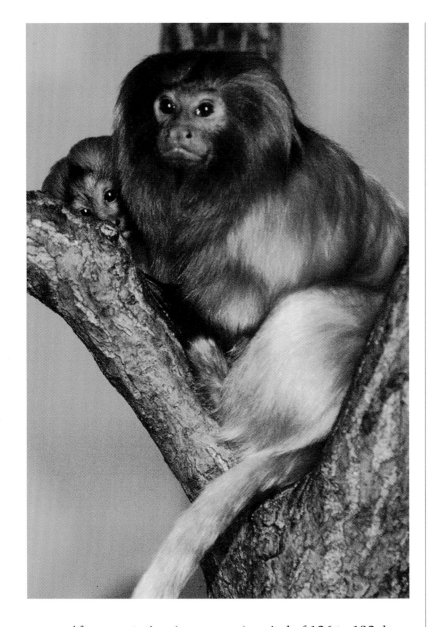

A golden lion tamarin perched on a tree branch. As tree dwellers, tamarins travel from tree to tree in search of food.

group. After a gestation (pregnancy) period of 126 to 132 days, female golden lion tamarins normally give birth to twins. Most births occur between September and March. Both mother and father share responsibility for raising their young.

Habitat and current distribution

The golden lion tamarin prefers to inhabit tropical forests along the Atlantic coast at altitudes below 1,300 to 1,600 feet

(396 to 488 meters). The animal is usually found 10 to 33 feet (3 to 10 meters) above the ground in trees where dense vines and interlacing branches provide cover.

The animal is limited to the Brazilian state of Rio de Janeiro. Biologists (people who study living organisms) estimate that no more than 550 golden lion tamarins currently exist in the wild.

History and conservation measures

The home of the golden lion tamarin is one of the most densely populated parts of Brazil. The major cause of the animal's decline has been—and continues to be—the clearing of its forest habitat. Trees are cut down to supply the lumber market and to create farmland and grazing land for domestic animals. As a result, only isolated pockets of forest provide suitable habitat for the golden lion tamarin. The animal is extremely endangered and on the brink of extinction.

The Poco D'Anta Reserve was established in Rio de Janeiro specifically to protect the golden lion tamarin. However, only a small percentage of the reserve contains suitable habitat. The animal has been bred in captivity and successfully reintroduced into former parts of its range. The National Zoo in Washington, D.C. and the Rio de Janeiro Primate Center have exchanged golden lion tamarins in an effort to prevent members of the same family from mating. This helps keep captive populations of the animal as genetically diverse as possible.

TAPIR, CENTRAL AMERICAN
Tapirus bairdii

PHYLUM: Chordata
CLASS: Mammalia
ORDER: Perissodactyla
FAMILY: Tapiridae
STATUS: Vulnerable, IUCN
Endangered, ESA
RANGE: Belize, Colombia, Costa
Rica, Ecuador, Guatemala,
Honduras, Mexico, Nicaragua,
Panama

Tapir, Central American
Tapirus bairdii

Description and biology

The Central American or Baird's tapir is a large animal with a medium to dark brown coat. Related to the horse and rhinoceros, it is almost as large as a donkey. An average Central American tapir has a head and body length of 6.5 to 8 feet (2 to 2.4 meters) and weighs between 550 and 660 pounds (250 and 300 kilograms). It stands 36 to 42 inches (91 to 107 centimeters) tall at its shoulder.

The animal has short legs and a stout body that narrows in front, which allows it to move quickly through the forest. A good swimmer, it spends much time in water or in mud. With small, deeply set eyes, the animal has poor vision, but its senses of hearing and smell are acute. Its nose and upper lip extend to form a short trunk, which the animal uses to

The Central American tapir shovels food into its mouth by extending its nose and upper lip to make a short trunk.

shovel food into its mouth. Its diet consists of grass, leaves, and a variety of fruit. Jaguars and mountain lions are the Central American tapir's main predators.

Male and female Central American tapirs mate at any time during the year. After a gestation (pregnancy) period of 390 to 405 days, a female tapir gives birth to a single calf. At birth, the calf is covered with protective colored markings that allow it to blend easily into its forest environment. These markings begin to fade within a few months. The calf may remain dependent on its mother for up to a year.

Habitat and current distribution

The Central American tapir is found from southern Mexico to northern Colombia. It lives in a variety of humid habitats, including marshes, mangrove swamps, and tropical rain forests. Biologists (people who study living organisms) do not know how many of the animals currently exist in the wild.

History and conservation measures

The Central American tapir once ranged as far south as Ecuador. In the past, the animal was hunted for its meat and hide and for sport. Now legally protected, the tapir nevertheless continues to be the target of poachers. Despite this problem, the most serious threat to the Central American tapir today is habitat destruction. Vast tracts of land in the animal's range have been cleared to create farmland to feed the growing human population in the area.

For the most part, the Central American tapir is now confined to reserves in Belize, Guatemala, Honduras, Nicaragua, Costa Rica, and Panama.

TIGER
Panthera tigris

PHYLUM: Chordata
CLASS: Mammalia
ORDER: Carnivora
FAMILY: Felidae
STATUS: Endangered, IUCN
Endangered, ESA
RANGE: Bangladesh, Bhutan,
Cambodia, China, India,
Indonesia, Laos, Malaysia,
Myanmar, Nepal, North Korea,
Russia, Thailand, Vietnam

Tiger
Panthera tigris

Description and biology

Tigers are members of the cat family. They are the biggest of the big cats, a group that includes leopards, lions, and jaguars. There are eight subspecies of tiger. Three of these—the Bali, Caspian, and Javan—all became extinct in the twentieth century. The remaining five subspecies are the Bengal (or Indian), Indo–Chinese, Siberian (or Amur), South Chinese, and Sumatran.

The color, size, and general appearance of tigers varies according to the subspecies. On average, a male tiger has a head and body length of 5 to 9 feet (1.5 to 2.7 meters) and a tail length of 2 to 3 feet (0.6 to 0.9 meter). It stands about 3.5 feet (1 meter) tall at its shoulder and weighs between 220 and 660 pounds (100 and 300 kilograms). Since the animal is found in a variety of climates, from the snowy forests of Siberia to

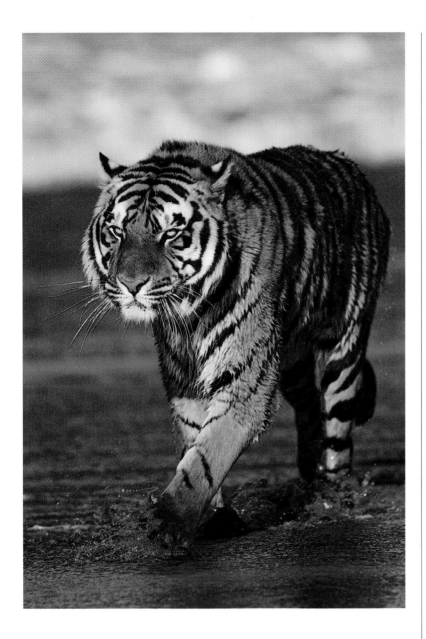

A Bengal tiger walking along a beach. Of the eight original subspecies of tiger only five remain. The Bengal tiger is one of these remaining subspecies.

the jungles of Indonesia, the length of its coat varies. In general, its coat is orange–yellow in color, with numerous black stripes. Its underparts are white. The striping pattern varies not only among subspecies but with each individual tiger.

Tigers are mainly nocturnal (active at night). They are able climbers, good swimmers, and fast runners. Tigers can leap up to 32 feet (10 meters) and swim up to 18 miles (29 kilometers). They are carnivores (meat–eaters), preying on deer, antelope, wild pigs, cattle, and other mammals. Their senses of hearing, sight, and smell are all keen. Tigers stalk or ambush their prey, pouncing on it from the rear or the side. The prey is usually killed by a bite to the neck or spine. Despite their abilities, tigers are successful hunters only about 10 percent of the time. Because of this, most tigers travel between 10 and 20 miles (16 and 32 kilometers) a night in search of food. Tigers that attack and eat humans are generally too old or sick to hunt wild animals.

Tigers are solitary animals with home ranges that vary between 4 and 1,500 square miles (10 and 3,885 square kilometers). They are not entirely loners, as they will band together to hunt and to share their kill. Males and females come together to mate at any time during the year, though primarily between November and April. After a gestation (pregnancy) period of just over 100 days, a female gives birth to a litter of two to four cubs. The cubs are blind and helpless for the first two weeks. They nurse for six to eight weeks, then begin accompanying their mother on hunting trips. After almost two years, they leave their mother's territory to establish their own.

Habitat and current distribution

Tigers occupy a wide variety of habitats, including rain forests, evergreen forests, mangrove swamps, marshlands, grasslands, and savannas.

There are currently as few as 5,500 tigers left in the wild. The Bengal tiger has the largest population of any tiger subspecies. Found in India, Bangladesh, Myanmar, Nepal, and Bhutan, it has an estimated population of about 3,750. The Indo–Chinese tiger is found in Laos, Malaysia, Thailand, Myanmar, and Vietnam. The South Chinese tiger, now almost extinct in the wild, is found only in southern China. The Siberian tiger, the largest of all subspecies, is found in North Korea, northern China, and the Amur–Ussuri region of Siberia in Russia. The Sumatran tiger, the smallest of all living tiger subspecies, is found on the island of Sumatra, Indonesia.

History and conservation measures

The protection of tigers has been an international concern since the 1970s, but the animals are still declining in number. At the beginning of the twentieth century, an estimated

100,000 tigers roamed the Asian forests and grasslands. That population has since decreased by about 95 percent. The Bali tiger, the smallest of the eight subspecies, became extinct in 1937. The Caspian tiger, once found as far west as Turkey, disappeared in the 1970s. The Javan tiger was last seen in 1983.

Historically, the tiger has been hunted as a trophy and for its beautiful coat. For centuries, many Asian cultures have used other tiger parts (bones, eyes, teeth, nails) in medicines, believing they cure diseases such as rheumatism and dysentery. Some people even believe that a soup made from the genitals of a male tiger can increase sexual ability. International treaties now protect tigers, but because of these ancient beliefs, the animals are still hunted and traded. Conservationists (people protecting the natural world) believe that two or three tigers are killed each day in China and Taiwan.

The primary threat to the tiger's current survival is habitat destruction. As forests throughout Asia are cleared for timber or to create farmland, tigers are forced into smaller and smaller areas. These tiny islands of forest do not hold enough prey for the animals, and they are forced to feed on livestock and even humans. Increased contact with humans has only resulted in more tiger deaths.

In 1972, the Indian government launched Project Tiger, a program that established 23 tiger reserves. Even though these reserves are patrolled by guards, poaching or illegal hunting still takes place.

Vicuña

Vicugna vicugna

Description and biology

The smallest member of the camel family, the vicuña is closely related to the llama and the alpaca. The color of the vicuña's soft and silky coat is light brown above and off–white below. A patch of longer hair covers the animal's throat and chest, keeping it warm when it rests on the ground. The vicuña has a small head in comparison with its body, and its eyes and ears are small and prominent. Its neck is long.

An average vicuña measures 4 to 6 feet (1.2 to 1.8 meters) in length and weighs 88 to 110 pounds (40 to 50 kilograms). It stands 30 to 40 inches (76 to 102 centimeters) tall at its shoulder. It feeds primarily on grasses, mosses, and other vegetation. Pumas and Andean foxes are its main predators.

A female vicuña and her young. It takes about a year for young vicuñas to become independent and leave their mothers.

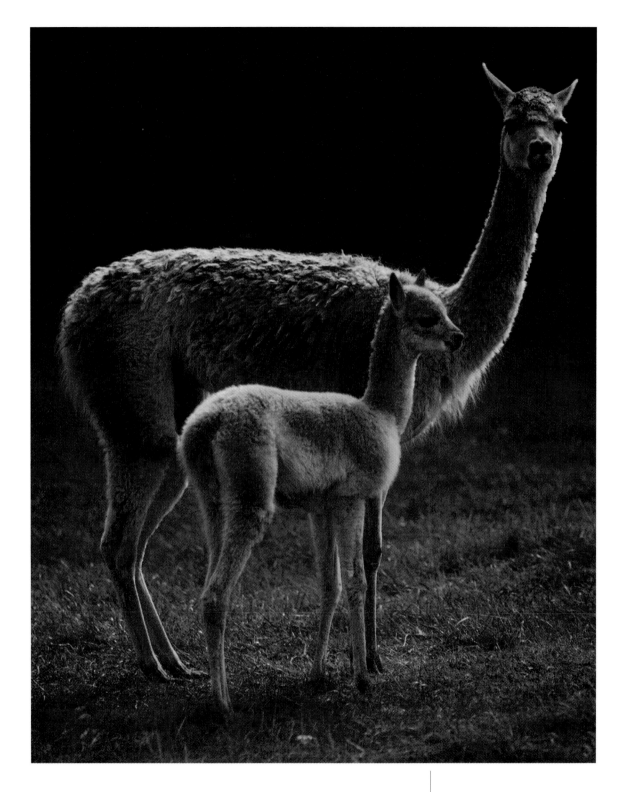

Vicuña are social animals. They form family groups consisting of a dominant male and a number of adult females with their young. The male defends a feeding and sleeping territory averaging 17 to 74 acres (7 to 30 hectares). Those males unable to defend a territory (and thus breed with females) live a solitary life or join other males to form bachelor groups.

Male and female vicuña mate in March or April. A female gives birth to one infant after a gestation (pregnancy) period of 330 to 350 days. The young vicuña nurses for up to ten months and becomes independent after about a year.

Habitat and current distribution

The vicuña is found in the central portion of the Andes Mountains in the South American countries of Argentina, Bolivia, Chile, and Peru. Biologists (people who study living organisms) estimate the current population to be over 100,000.

The vicuña prefers to inhabit semiarid (semidry) grasslands and plateaus at elevations of 9,850 to 15,100 feet (3,000 to 4,600 meters). Groups spend the day in one feeding territory, then move at night to a territory at a higher elevation to sleep.

History and conservation measures

Because of its lustrous wool—often said to be among the finest in the world—the vicuña has been sought since the days of the Inca, native Quechuan people of Peru who established an empire in South America in the fifteenth century. The Inca pursued the animal not to kill it, but to shear its wool, which was then made into certain types of ritual clothing. When Spanish explorers (conquistadors) conquered the Inca in the sixteenth century, they began to hunt the vicuña without care.

Before they became the target of hunters, as many as several million vicuña may have existed. By the time of the conquistadors, the animal's population had been reduced to less than 500,000. By 1965, only 6,500 vicuña survived.

Although international treaties now ban the taking of the vicuña, illegal hunting is still a problem in parts of the animal's range, particularly in Peru and Bolivia. However, the majority of vicuña currently live on protected reserves.

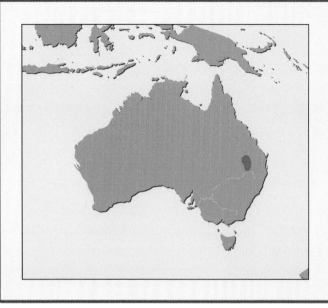

WALLABY, BRINDLED NAIL–TAILED
Onychogalea fraenata

PHYLUM: Chordata
CLASS: Mammalia
ORDER: Marsupialia
FAMILY: Macropodidae
STATUS: Endangered, IUCN
Endangered, ESA
RANGE: Australia

Wallaby, brindled nail–tailed

Onychogalea fraenata

Description and biology

A member of the kangaroo family, the brindled nail–tailed wallaby gets its name from its silver–gray coat with dark flecks ("brindled") and from the horny spur on the end of its tail ("nail–tailed"). An average brindled nail–tailed wallaby has a head and body length of 17.5 to 23.5 inches (44.5 to 59.7 centimeters) and weighs about 11 pounds (5 kilograms). Its tail is almost as long as its body, measuring 13.5 to 19.5 inches (34.3 to 49.5 centimeters).

This wallaby is a solitary animal that rests in a shallow depression under a shrub, tree, or log during the day. At night, it feeds on a variety of grasses and herbs. Dingoes, wild Australian dogs, are the animal's main predator.

Wallabies are marsupials, or mammals whose young continue to develop after birth in a pouch on the outside of the

183

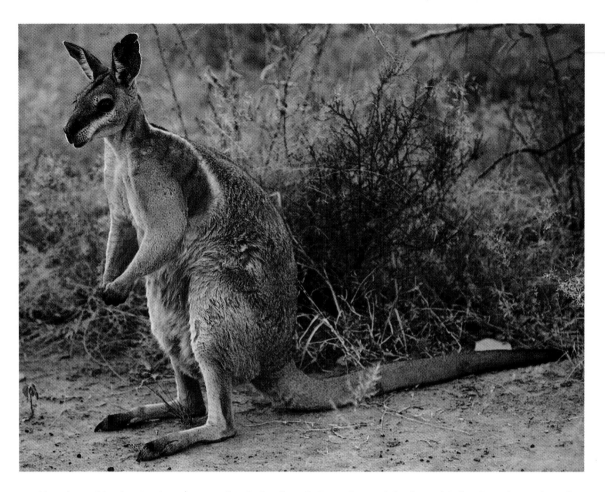

mother's body. Other than this fact, biologists (people who study living organisms) know very little about the breeding habits of this particular species of wallaby.

Habitat and current distribution

The only population of brindled nail–tailed wallabies is near the town of Dingo in the northeastern Australian state of Queensland. In the early 1980s, biologists estimated that their population numbered 800.

During the day, brindled nail–tailed wallabies prefer to inhabit forest areas dominated by trees or shrubs. At night, they feed in open woodland or grassland areas.

History and conservation measures

The brindled nail–tailed wallaby was once common throughout eastern and southeastern Australia. In the early

1800s, farmers and ranchers moved into the animal's range, bringing with them domestic livestock. The brindled nail–tailed wallaby was then forced to compete for food with these grazing animals, especially sheep. The farmers and ranchers soon considered the wallaby a pest and began paying to have the animal killed. By 1930, it was considered extinct.

In 1973, a small population of brindled nail–tailed wallabies was discovered near the town of Dingo. Later that decade, the Taunton Scientific Reserve was established to protect this new population. The majority of surviving brindled nail–tailed wallabies now exist there.

WHALE, BLUE
Balaenoptera musculus

PHYLUM: Chordata

CLASS: Mammalia

ORDER: Cetacea

FAMILY: Balaenopteridae

STATUS: Endangered, IUCN
Endangered, ESA

RANGE: Oceanic

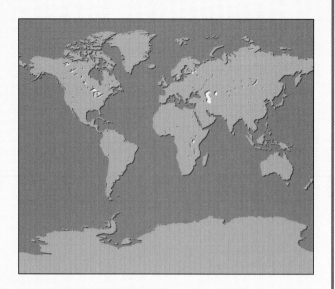

Whale, blue

Balaenoptera musculus

Description and biology

Scientists consider the blue whale to be the largest animal that has ever lived on Earth. An average adult measures 79 to 88 feet (24 to 27 meters) long and weighs between 130 and 150 tons (118 and 136 metric tons). In the past, some blue whales reached a length of 100 feet (30 meters). Now, the animals seldom grow that large because of extensive whaling (the hunting of whales). The blue whale has a wide, U–shaped head and a dorsal (on its back) fin. Its body is slate blue in color. Sometimes, microorganisms accumulate on the whale's body, giving it a faintly yellow sheen. This is why it is also called the sulfur–bottomed whale.

The blue whale feeds mainly on krill, which are small, shrimplike shellfish. Like all whales in its family, the blue whale uses the fringed baleen (whalebone) plates that line its mouth to strain krill from seawater. The animal has 80 to 100 furrows (called ventral grooves) lining its narrow neck. When it sucks in seawater, the grooves allow its throat to expand

The fin of a blue whale. Scientists consider the whale to be the largest animal to ever live on the Earth.

like a pouch. As it expels the large volume of water from its mouth, its baleen plates trap the krill.

Blue whales mate at the end of winter. After a gestation (pregnancy) period of 300 to 330 days, a female blue whale gives birth to one calf, which measures 20 to 23 feet (6 to 7 meters) long. The calf nurses for up to seven months.

Habitat and current distribution

Blue whales are found in all of the major oceans. Most blue whales prefer cold waters and open seas. In summer, they inhabit arctic and Antarctic waters, feeding on krill in the water of melting ice packs. In winter, they migrate to warmer waters near the equator, where they will mate. Some blue whales, however, do not appear to migrate, residing year–round in tropical coastal areas. Such whales have been observed off the coast of Peru and in the northern Indian Ocean.

Scientists estimate that less than 2,000 blue whales currently exist in the world's oceans.

History and conservation measures

When large–scale whaling began in the seventeenth century, blue whales were considered too difficult to hunt because of their size, speed, and strength. This view changed in the mid–nineteenth century with the development of the exploding–head harpoon and the factory ship (which could completely process whales caught at sea). Blue whales were now a prime prey, and their numbers decreased drastically, especially in the twentieth century. Between 1920 and 1970, an estimated 280,000 blue whales were slaughtered.

In 1964, the International Whaling Commission (IWC; body that regulates most of the world's whaling activity) banned the hunting of blue whales. However, various nations defy the rulings of the IWC. The blue whale and other whales continue to be hunted.

The blue whale also faces the loss of its main food source, krill. Scientists have discovered that the krill population has decreased by almost 90 percent since 1980. Krill feed on algae that grow underneath sea ice. As temperatures have risen in Antarctica in the last 20 years, melting a sizable portion of sea ice, the algae population has diminished. In a domino effect, this loss could affect the entire Antarctic food chain. Some scientists believe this situation is the result of global warming—the rise in Earth's temperature that is attributed to the buildup of carbon dioxide and other pollutants in the atmosphere.

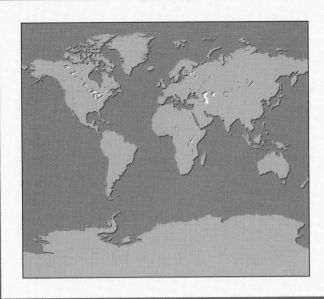

WHALE, HUMPBACK
Megaptera novaeangliae

PHYLUM: Chordata

CLASS: Mammalia

ORDER: Cetacea

FAMILY: Balaenopteridae

STATUS: Vulnerable, IUCN
Endangered, ESA

RANGE: Oceanic

Whale, humpback

Megaptera novaeangliae

Description and biology

The humpback whale is most known for its acrobatic leaps and for its distinctive pattern of sounds, called songs. An average humpback whale has a head and body length of 42 to 52 feet (13 to 16 meters) and weighs between 30 and 60 tons (27 and 54 metric tons). Its winglike pectoral (chest or side) fins measure 13 to 16 feet (4 to 5 meters) long. While the whale's upper body is dark gray, its underparts are lighter. White patterns mark the pectoral fins. Despite the animal's large size, it is able to breach (leap out of the water) and perform spectacular spins.

The diet of humpback whales includes herring, pink salmon, Arctic cod, certain mollusks, krill (small, shrimplike shellfish), and other small fishes. Those humpback whales inhabiting Antarctic waters feed primarily on krill. The whales have brushlike plates of baleen (whalebone) lining the roofs of their mouths. Their narrow throats are lined with furrows

A humpback whale comes to the surface for air. Although there is a ban on hunting the whales, illegal hunting still continues.

(called ventral grooves). To feed, the whales suck in large amounts of water, and the furrows allow their throats to expand like a pouch. The animals then expel the water through their baleen plates, straining out any food.

Large schools of humpback whales form when they migrate between cold and warm waters. Humpback whales inhabiting the waters of the Northern Hemisphere mate between October and March; those in the Southern Hemisphere mate between April and September. A female humpback whale gives birth to a single calf after a gestation (pregnancy) period of about one year. The calf nurses for about one year afterward.

Although scientists are not sure why, male humpback whales emit their haunting song during the mating season. All males in the same group "sing" the same song, composed of moans, cries, grunts, snores, and chirps. Scientists began recording humpback whale songs in the early 1950s. They have found that the songs change each year and no two songs have ever been the same.

Habitat and current distribution

Humpback whales are found in all oceans on Earth from the Arctic to the Antarctic. They feed in colder waters during spring, summer, and autumn. In winter, they migrate to warmer waters near the equator, swimming in deep water along coastlines. Scientists estimate that 25,000 humpback whales currently exist.

History and conservation measures

About 150,000 humpback whales probably existed worldwide when large–scale whaling (whale hunting) began in the seventeenth century. Whales have been hunted for their oil, which is extracted from their blubber and other body parts. Whale oil was originally used in oil lamps. Today, it is used in soap-making, as a dressing for leather, and as a lubricant. Over the centuries, many carvings and items of jewelry—called scrimshaw—have been made from baleen.

With improved hunting techniques in the nineteenth century (including the development of the exploding–head harpoon), the number of humpback whales quickly declined. By the early twentieth century, the population of whales in the North Atlantic had been depleted. Whalers then began hunting those whales inhabiting the Pacific Ocean and the waters of the Southern Hemisphere.

The International Whaling Commission (IWC; body that regulates most of the world's whaling activity) banned the hunting of humpback whales in 1963. However, some nations disregard the decrees of the IWC and the hunting of protected whales continues. Because humpback whales travel close to shore, they are also threatened by shoreline pollution, boat traffic, and fishing nets.

WOLF, GRAY
Canis lupus

PHYLUM: Chordata
CLASS: Mammalia
ORDER: Carnivora
FAMILY: Canidae
STATUS: Lower risk: conservation dependent, IUCN
Endangered, ESA
RANGE: Canada, USA

Wolf, gray
Canis lupus

Description and biology

The North American gray wolf, also known as the timber wolf, is the largest member of the canidae (dog) family. An average adult measures 5 to 6 feet (1.5 to 1.8 meters) from nose to tail, and stands 26 to 32 inches (66 to 81 centimeters) at its shoulder. It can weigh between 70 and 110 pounds (32 and 50 kilograms). Females are slightly smaller than males. The wolf's coat is usually tan or a grizzled gray and black. Some wolves are all black or all white.

The gray wolf is well–adapted for hunting. It has long legs and keen senses of hearing and smell. The wolf is a carnivore or meat–eater. It feeds on a variety of mammals from large

A howling gray wolf. Conservation efforts to protect this animal have been so successful, that the gray wolf may be taken off the Endangered Species List over some its range.

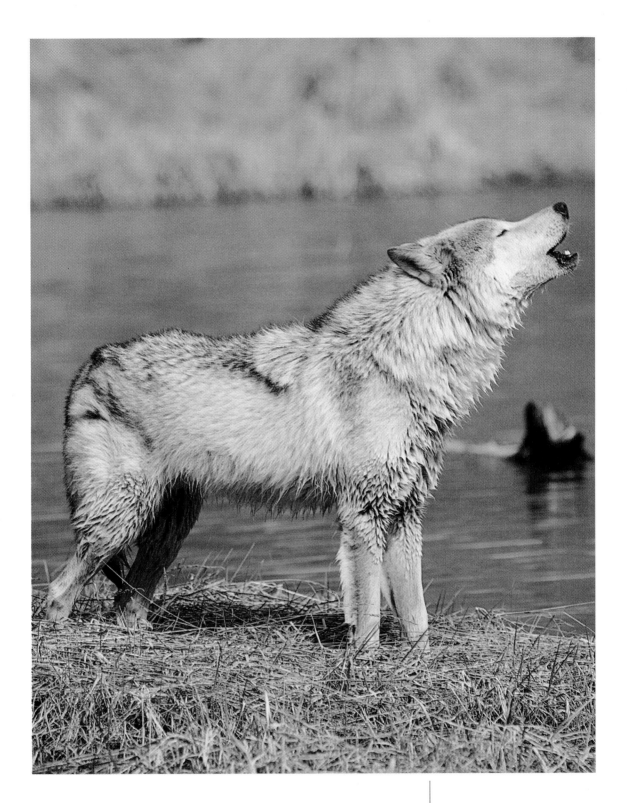

hoofed animals such as elk and deer to smaller animals such as beavers and rabbits. It will also eat small rodents like mice. Wolves generally kill animals that are young, old, diseased, or deformed—those that are easy to capture. However, if the opportunity arises, the wolf will kill a healthy animal.

Wolves live in packs or family groups typically composed of a set of parents, their offspring, and other nonbreeding adults. The social structure within a pack is complex. The dominant male and female are both called alphas, but they may not mate with each other. The alpha female, who has the dominant role in the pack, will sometimes mate with a superior male (or superior males) in the pack. The hierarchy (pronounced HIGH–a–rar–key) or ranking of dominant and subordinate animals within a pack help it function as a unit.

The packs generally hunt within a specific territory. Territories may be as large as 50 square miles (130 square kilometers) or even extend to 1,000 square miles (2,590 square kilometers), depending on available food. Wolves communicate with fellow pack–mates and other wolf packs through facial and body postures, scent markings (urine and feces), and vocalizations, which include barks, whimpers, growls, and howls.

Gray wolves begin mating when they are two to three years old. A females digs a den or uses an existing shelter or structure in which to rear her pups for the first six weeks of their lives. In early spring, she gives birth to an average litter of six pups. The pups depend completely on their mother's milk for the first month, then they are gradually weaned off the mother's milk. By seven to eight months of age, when they are almost fully grown, the young wolves begin hunting with the adults. Often after one or two years of age, a young wolf will leave and try to form its own pack.

Habitat and current distribution

In North America, the gray wolf is found in wilderness forests and tundra areas of northern Canada and the United States (gray wolves are also found in small pockets in Europe, Asia, and the Middle East). A subspecies of the gray wolf, the Mexican gray wolf, once inhabited Mexico and the southwestern United States.

In the United States, the gray wolf is found primarily in Alaska (listed as neither endangered nor threatened) and Minnesota (listed as threatened). Where it is found in other parts of the United States—Idaho, Michigan, Montana, Wisconsin, Wyoming, and possibly Washington—it is listed as endangered.

Approximately 50,000 wolves remain in Canada and 7,500 to 10,500 in the United States (5,000 to 8,000 of which are in Alaska). Some 150,000 remain elsewhere in the world.

History and conservation measures

Gray wolves once lived everywhere north of about 20° latitude, a parallel that runs through Mexico City and southern India. They occupied an array of climates and ecosystems (ecological community consisting of living things and their environment), from dry deserts to deciduous (tree or plants that shed) forests to frozen tundra. On the North American continent, they ranged from coast to coast and from Canada to Mexico.

As settlers moved west across America in the nineteenth century, they killed off most of the populations of bison, deer, elk, and moose—animals that were important prey for wolves. With little natural prey left, wolves then turned to sheep and cattle. To protect livestock, ranchers and government agencies began a decades–long campaign to eliminate the animals. Wolves were trapped, shot, and hunted with dogs. Animal carcasses (dead bodies) salted with strychnine (pronounced STRICK–nine; a poison) were left out for wolves to eat. Unfortunately, this practice killed eagles, ravens, foxes, bears, and other animals that also fed on the poisoned carcasses. By the late 1920s, no wolves were left in Yellowstone National Park.

At present, gray wolves occupy just 6 percent of their former range in the contiguous United States (connected 48 states). In 1995 and 1996, the U.S. government relocated about 65 gray wolves from Canada to Yellowstone National Park and central Idaho. The wolves adjusted quickly. Within two years, they had reshaped the Yellowstone ecosystem, improving the overall balance of species in the park. The wolves killed many of the park's coyotes, which allowed the rodent population to increase. This, in turn, allowed animals that feed on rodents to increase in number. Other animals, such as grizzly bears, benefitted by feeding on the remains of elk killed by wolves.

From the beginning, however, ranchers and farm groups have opposed wolf reintroduction efforts, asserting that wolves are a threat to livestock in the area. To ease the concerns of ranchers, the U.S. government downgraded the wolves' status in Yellowstone and Idaho from "endangered" to "threatened." This change gave ranchers the legal right to shoot any wolves attacking their livestock.

This compromise was still not enough for some livestock groups. They sued to stop the reintroduction efforts. Certain environmental groups, including the Audubon Society, also filed a suit against the government to stop the reintroduction. They wanted to keep full "endangered" status for the two or three wolves already living in central Idaho.

In December 1997, a federal judge ruled that the government had violated parts of the Endangered Species Act when it reintroduced wolves to Yellowstone. The judge did stay (delay) his decision, allowing federal agencies and other environmental groups time to file an appeal. If the judge's decision is upheld, all of the gray wolves in Yellowstone (a population of about 160) will have to be killed.

Gray wolves in the midwestern section of the country—Michigan, Minnesota, and Wisconsin—have fared much better. In May 1998, U.S. Interior Secretary Bruce Babbitt proposed that their status on the Endangered Species List be changed (they were one of 29 species that would be either downgraded or removed completely from the list). Just one month later, Babbitt decided that the gray wolves in those states—numbering about 2,500—should be removed completely from protection under the Endangered Species Act. The authority to manage these wolf populations would be handled by the states themselves.

At the same time, Babbitt also proposed that gray wolves in Montana, Wyoming, and parts of Idaho be reclassified to threatened from endangered. Although their populations were still small, the wolves were increasing in number in that part of the country. The move would give wildlife officials more control in managing the wolves in that area.

The change in the wolves' legal status would probably not take effect for at least six months. The new policies would also not affect the protection afforded gray wolves inhabiting Yellowstone National Park or central Idaho.

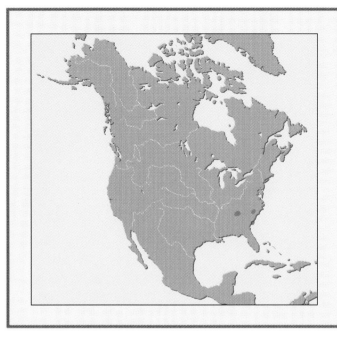

WOLF, RED
Canis rufus

PHYLUM: Chordata
CLASS: Mammalia
ORDER: Carnivora
FAMILY: Canidae
STATUS: Critically endangered, IUCN
Endangered, ESA
RANGE: USA (reintroduced in North Carolina and Tennessee)

Wolf, red
Canis rufus

Description and biology

Although called the red wolf, the animal's coat varies in color from cinnamon–brown to nearly black. Smaller than its relative the gray wolf, the red wolf is about the size of a large dog. It has an average head and body length of 37 to 47 inches (94 to 119 centimeters) and a tail length of about 10 inches (25 centimeters). It weighs between 45 and 65 pounds (20 and 30 kilograms). The animal's most distinguishing features are its long ears and legs.

The red wolf feeds on swamp rabbits, raccoons, birds, white–tailed deer, and other small mammals. It is also known to eat chickens and, sometimes, calves and piglets. A male and female pair hunts on a territory averaging 30 to 40 square miles (78 to 104 square kilometers).

The wolves have a complex social order made up of family groups called packs. Individual males and females form a

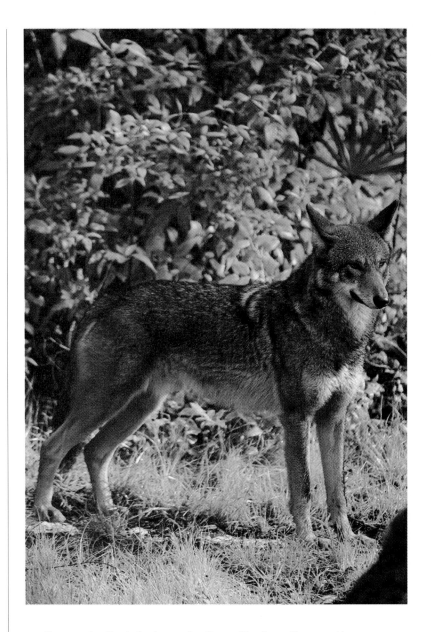

mating pair that is long–lasting. During the mating season (January to April), the pair establishes a den, usually in hollow logs, ditch banks, or under rock outcrops. Here they raise their young year after year. A female red wolf gives birth to a litter of two to eight pups after a gestation (pregnancy) period of 61 to 63 days. The pups, who are born with their eyes closed, are completely dependent on their mother for the first two months. They remain with their parents for about two to three years.

Habitat and current distribution

The red wolf has been declared biologically extinct in the wild. All the animals currently in existence were raised in captivity. In 1987, a small population of captive–bred red wolves was reintroduced into the wild in North Carolina. Another small group was reintroduced into the Great Smoky Mountains National Park in Tennessee in 1992.

The animals prefer to inhabit swamps, wetlands, bushlands, and forests.

History and conservation measures

The red wolf once ranged from central Texas east to the Atlantic coast and from the Gulf of Mexico north to southern Pennsylvania. In the early twentieth century, it began disappearing from much of that range. By the middle of the century, only scattered populations of the animal survived. Its decline was brought about by human settlers moving into its habitat. Forests were cleared for their timber or to create farmland, and the settlers killed the red wolf out of fear and ignorance.

As forests were cut down in eastern Texas and Oklahoma, the separate ranges of the red wolf and the coyote began to meet. The red wolves, whose numbers were very low, started to interbreed with the coyotes. As a result, the number of genetically pure red wolves in the wild became even smaller.

In 1973, the U.S. Fish and Wildlife Service (USFWS) established a captive breeding program in hopes of reintroducing the red wolf into the wild. It was the first recovery plan developed by the USFWS for an endangered species. Over a six–year period, over 400 animals believed to be red wolves were captured in the wild. Only 17 of those were found to be true red wolves, and only 14 of these were able to breed successfully in captivity.

In 1987, four pairs of captive–bred red wolves were reintroduced to the wild on the 120,000–acre Alligator River National Wildlife Refuge in northeastern North Carolina. Although disease and conflicts with humans took its toll on this small population, wild births and additional releases of captive–bred animals have kept it going. Today, there are more than 50 red wolves in this refuge.

Beginning in 1989, the USFWS established island sites where captive–bred wolves can have their first experience in the wild without having much human contact. Cape Romain National Wildlife Refuge on Bull Island, South Carolina; Gulf Islands National Seashore on Horn Island, Mississippi; and St. Vincent National Wildlife Refuge on St. Vincent, Florida are the three pre–reintroduction sites. The red wolves are allowed to breed and roam freely on these islands. After a while, they are captured and taken to the Alligator River refuge or the Great Smoky Mountain National Park.

Red wolves are bred in 31 facilities across the United States. There are between 250 and 300 red wolves currently in existence, two–thirds of which are in captivity.

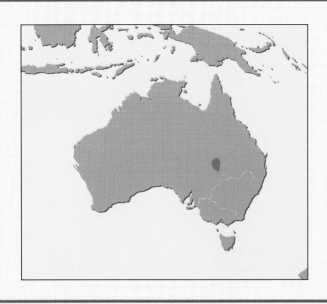

WOMBAT, NORTHERN HAIRY–NOSED
Lasiorhinus krefftii

PHYLUM: Chordata

CLASS: Mammalia

ORDER: Marsupialia

FAMILY: Vombatidae

STATUS: Critically endangered, IUCN
Endangered, ESA

RANGE: Australia

Wombat, northern hairy–nosed

Lasiorhinus krefftii

Description and biology

The northern hairy–nosed wombat is also variously known as the Queensland hairy–nosed wombat or Barnard's hairy–nosed wombat. The animal does, indeed, have a hairy nose or muzzle. Its body is covered with a soft, silky brown coat. It has a large head, small eyes, pointed ears, and powerful legs with strong claws. The animal's poor eyesight is offset by its keen senses of hearing and smell. An average northern hairy–nosed wombat has a stocky body measuring 3.25 feet (1 meter) in length and weighing between 42 and 70 pounds (19 and 32 kilograms).

The animal uses its strong foreclaws to excavate a series of connected burrows called a warren. Each burrow may be 100 feet (30.5 meters) long, and each warren may have several entrances. The animal's home range surrounding its war-

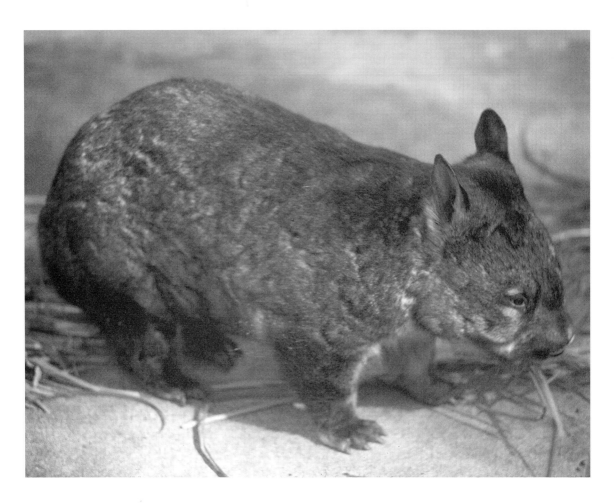

A northern hairy–nosed wombat. The wombat is considered rare since its current population only numbers 65.

ren may extend over 14.8 acres (6 hectares). The northern hairy–nosed wombat feeds at night on grass, especially bunch speargrass.

The northern hairy–nosed wombat belongs to an order of mammals known as marsupials, whose young continue to develop after birth in a pouch on the outside of the mother's body. After a female northern hairy–nosed wombat gives birth to a single infant in summer (November to March), she carries her infant in her pouch for about six months. The young wombat nurses for almost nine months.

Habitat and current distribution

The northern hairy–nosed wombat prefers to inhabit open, semiarid (semidry) woodlands or grasslands. It generally digs its burrows in sandy soils that are supported by tree roots.

The only known surviving population of northern hairy–nosed wombats is found in the Epping Forest National Park in the northeastern Australian state of Queensland. Biologists (people who study living organisms) estimate that their population numbers 65.

History and conservation measures

The northern hairy–nosed wombat was probably already quite rare when Europeans began settling in Australia in the late eighteenth century. By 1909, it was considered extinct. In 1937, however, a small group of the animals was discovered west of the city of Clermont in east–central Queensland.

The area inhabited by these remaining wombats was declared a national park in the 1970s. At first, the animals were not fully protected, as cattle in the park grazed on the wombat's food source. Although steps have been taken since then to eliminate cattle from the park, the number of surviving northern hairy–nosed wombats continues to be very low.

YAK, WILD
Bos grunniens mutus

PHYLUM: Chordata
CLASS: Mammalia
ORDER: Artiodactyla
FAMILY: Bovidae
STATUS: Vulnerable, IUCN
Endangered, ESA
RANGE: China, India, Nepal

Yak, wild
Bos grunniens mutus

Description and biology

The wild yak is a rare and mysterious animal. Its huge body is covered with coarse, shaggy, dark brown hair that hangs almost to the ground. Its muzzle is white. The animal has a large, drooping head, humped shoulders, and short legs. The average male wild yak has a head and body length of 10.75 feet (3.3 meters) and stands 5.5 to 6.5 feet (1.7 to 2 meters) tall at its shoulder. It weighs between 1,800 and 2,200 pounds (820 and 1,000 kilograms). Its upward curved horns are dark and may grow up to 3 feet (0.9 meter) long. Females are substantially smaller.

Wild yaks feed on mosses and lichens (organisms composed of a fungus and an alga) while inhabiting areas at high elevations. At lower elevations, they feed on mosses, herbs, and grasses. Because vegetation is often scarce in their habitat, the animals often cover great distances looking for food. A known predator is the Tibetan wolf.

Males and females form separate herds. During mating season, which begins in September, the herds come together and the males compete with each other over the right to mate with available females. After a gestation (pregnancy) period of 258 days, a female wild yak gives birth to a single calf. The calf then nurses for up to a year.

Habitat and current distribution

Although there are millions of domesticated yaks in the world today, only a few hundred wild yaks exist. They inhabit isolated patches on the Tibetan Plateau at elevations between 13,500 and 20,000 feet (4,115 and 6,096 meters).

History and conservation measures

The wild yak's range once extended into northern Siberia. Biologists (people who study living organisms) believe the an-

Because enforcement of the laws protecting the wild yak is difficult, the few hundred existing animals remain in serious danger of extinction.

imal's population was still quite large at the beginning of the twentieth century. Since that time, excessive hunting has reduced the number of wild yaks to a dangerously low level. Humans have always valued the animal's meat, hide, and coat. Even though the wild yak is protected by international treaties, hunting continues. The Chinese government has been guilty of allowing foreign hunters to kill the animals for sport.

Because of the wild yak's remote mountain habitat, the enforcement of existing laws and the development of conservation plans is almost impossible. As a result, the surviving animals remain in grave danger.

ZEBRA, GREVY'S
Equus grevyi

PHYLUM: Chordata
CLASS: Mammalia
ORDER: Perissodactyla
FAMILY: Equidae
STATUS: Endangered, IUCN
Threatened, ESA
RANGE: Ethiopia, Kenya

Zebra, Grevy's

Equus grevyi

Description and biology

A member of the horse family, the Grevy's zebra is similar in appearance to a mule. It has an average head and body length of 8 to 10 feet (2.4 to 3 meters) and a shoulder height of 4.5 to 5 feet (1.4 to 1.5 meters). It weighs between 800 and 950 pounds (360 and 430 kilograms). The animal has a large head, rounded ears, a tufted tail, and a short, stiff mane. It feeds primarily on grass. Lions, hyenas, and crocodiles are the Grevy's zebra's main predators.

A beautiful pattern of narrow black and white vertical stripes covers most of the Grevy's zebra's head and body. A dark stripe runs down the top of its back. Its belly is white. Scientists once thought that the stripes on zebras served to camouflage or protect the animals from predators. Some researchers now believe the stripes help the animals recog-

Some scientists now believe that Grevy's zebra's black–and–white stripes help it to distinguish other members of its group.

nize other members of their group and, thus, form social bonds.

Grevy's zebras are unique among zebras in that they do not form permanent groups. Nursing females and their foals (young), other females, and solitary males sometimes gather in temporary herds. Some males establish territories ranging between 1 and 4 square miles (2.6 and 10.4 square kilometers) and will compete with other males over the right to mate with females in their territory. Mating takes place any time of the year, but peaks in mid–summer and mid–fall. After a gestation (pregnancy) period of 390 days, a female Grevy's zebra gives birth to a single foal. The newborn foal is brown and black in color, and its mane extends down its back to its tail. After four months, it develops adult coloring. The foal may remain with its mother for up to three years.

Habitat and current distribution

Grevy's zebras inhabit the semiarid (semidry) scrublands and grasslands in southern Ethiopia and Kenya. Although unsure of the total number of Grevy's zebras currently in existence, scientists believe that number is declining.

History and conservation measures

Between the late 1970s and late 1980s, the Grevy's zebra population decreased by 70 percent. Once populous in Somalia, the animal is now extinct there. Hunting for its beautiful skin was the main reason for its decline in early years. The animal is now legally protected, and poaching (illegal hunting) is not considered a major problem.

The principal current threat to the Grevy's zebra is the loss of its habitat. Increasing numbers of domestic livestock now graze on the animal's food source. Much of the water that flowed through its semiarid habitat in Kenya has been diverted to irrigate nearby developing farmland.

Further Research

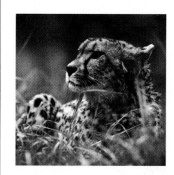

Books

Ackerman, Diane. *The Rarest of the Rare: Vanishing Animals, Timeless Worlds.* New York: Random House, 1995. Naturalist and poet Ackerman travels from the Amazon rain forests to a remote Japanese island in search of endangered creatures and their habitats, revealing the factors that are contributing to their endangerment and describing preservation efforts.

Baillie, Jonathan, and Brian Groombridge, eds. *1996 IUCN Red List of Threatened Animals.* Gland, Switzerland: IUCN–The World Conservation Union, 1996. An extensive listing of endangered and threatened animal species, providing scientifically based information on the status of those species at a global level.

Baskin, Yvonne. *The Work of Nature: How the Diversity of Life Sustains Us.* Washington, DC: Island Press, 1997. Science writer Baskin examines the practical consequences of declining biodiversity on ecosystem health and functioning, highlighting examples from around the world.

Chadwick, Douglas W., and Joel Sartore. *The Company We Keep: America's Endangered Species.* Washington, DC: National Geographic Society, 1996. Wildlife biologist Chadwick chronicles past and current conservation efforts, profiling dozens of birds and animals on the top ten endangered list. The book, for readers aged ten and above, also includes rich photographs by photojournalist Sartore, range maps, habitat descriptions, population counts, and current status for all endangered North American species.

Cohen, Daniel. *The Modern Ark: Saving Endangered Species.* New York: Putnam, 1995. Aimed at young adult readers, this work explains the problems faced by endangered species and the solutions—such as the Species Survival Plan—to help protect their futures.

Dobson, David. *Can We Save Them? Endangered Species of North America.* Watertown, MA: Charlesbridge, 1997. For students aged seven to ten, Dobson's work introduces readers to twelve species of endangered animals and plants in North America and suggests ways to restore each one's natural environment.

Earle, Sylvia. *Sea Change: A Message of the Oceans.* New York: Putnam, 1995. Marine biologist and leading deep–sea explorer Earle writes about her three decades of undersea exploration and makes an urgent plea for the preservation of the world's fragile and rapidly deteriorating ocean ecosystems.

Endangered Wildlife of the World. New York: Marshall Cavendish, 1993. Developed for young adults, this 11–volume reference set presents 1,400 alphabetical entries focusing on the plight of endangered species, with a special emphasis placed on the species of North America.

Galan, Mark. *There's Still Time: The Success of the Endangered Species Act.* Washington, DC: National Geographic Society, 1997. For young readers, this photo–essay work features plants and animals that have been brought back from the brink of extinction, primarily because of the Endangered Species Act.

Hoff, Mary King, and Mary M. Rodgers. *Our Endangered Planet: Life on Land.* Minneapolis, MN: Lerner, 1992. For young adult readers, Hoff's work describes the delicate ecological balance among all living things on land, the damage done by humanity in contributing to the extinction of various species, and ways of preventing further harm.

Hoyt, John Arthur. *Animals in Peril: How "Sustainable Use" Is Wiping Out the World's Wildlife.* New York: Avery Publishing Group, 1995. Hoyt, executive officer of the U.S. Humane Society, contends that conservation agencies are destroying many animal species by cooperating with local governments in a conservation policy that actually promotes slaughter, suffering, and extinction.

Mann, Charles, and Mark Plummer. *Noah's Choice: The Future of Endangered Species.* New York: Knopf, 1995. Mann and Plummer examine the controversy over the Endangered Species Act and call for a new set of principles to serve as a guideline for choosing which endangered species to save.

Matthiessen, Peter. *Wildlife in America.* Rev. ed. New York: Penguin Books, 1995. Acclaimed naturalist–writer Matthiessen first published this classic work on the history of the rare, threatened, and extinct animals of North America in 1959.

McClung, Robert. *Last of the Wild: Vanished and Vanishing Giants of the Animal World.* Hamden, CT: Linnet Books, 1997. For readers aged 12 and above, McClung's work profiles threatened animals around the world and discusses why they are in danger and what is being done to save them.

McClung, Robert. *Lost Wild America: The Story of Our Extinct and Vanishing Wildlife.* Hamden, CT: Shoe String Press, 1993. McClung traces the history of wildlife conservation and environmental politics in America to 1992, and describes various extinct or endangered species.

Meacham, Cory J. *How the Tiger Lost Its Stripes: An Exploration into the Endangerment of a Species.* New York: Harcourt Brace, 1997. Journalist Meacham offers a probing analysis of the endangerment of the world's pure species of tigers and the role of zoos, scientists, and politics in stopping it.

Middleton, Susan, and David Liittschwager. *Witness: Endangered Species of North America.* San Francisco, CA: Chronicle Books, 1994. Through a series of 200 color and duotone portraits, photographers Middleton and Liittschwager capture 100 species of North American animals and plants on the brink of extinction.

Patent, Dorothy Hinshaw. *Back to the Wild.* San Diego, CA: Gulliver Books, 1997. For readers aged ten and above, Patent's work describes efforts to save endangered animals from extinction by breeding them in captivity, teaching them survival skills, and then releasing them into the wild.

Pollock, Stephen Thomas. *The Atlas of Endangered Animals.* New York: Facts on File, 1993. For younger readers, Pollock's work uses maps, pictures, symbols, and text to focus on areas of the world in which human activity is threatening to destroy already endangered animal species.

Quammen, David. *The Song of the Dodo: Island Biogeography in an Age of Extinctions.* New York: Scribner, 1996. In a work for adult readers, Quammen interweaves personal observation, scientific theory, and history to examine the mysteries of evolution and extinction as they have been illuminated by the study of islands.

Schaller, George. *The Last Panda.* Chicago, IL: University of Chicago Press, 1993. Noted biologist Schaller presents an account of the four years he spent in China's Sichuan Province working to protect both panda habitat and the few pandas that remained.

Tudge, Colin. *Last Animals at the Zoo: How Mass Extinctions Can Be Stopped.* Washington, DC: Island Press, 1992. Zoologist Tudge details the grim conditions many animals must overcome in their natural habitats and the bleak prospects for recovery by those already on the brink of extinction.

Walter, Kerry S., and Harriet Gillett, eds. *1997 IUCN Red List of Threatened Plants.* Gland, Switzerland: IUCN–The World Conservation Union, 1998. An extensive listing of endangered and threatened plant species, providing scientifically based information on the status of those species at a global level.

Periodicals

Endangered Species Bulletin
  Division of Endangered Species
  U.S. Fish and Wildlife Service, Washington, DC 20240

Endangered Species UPDATE
  School of Natural Resources and Environment
  The University of Michigan, Ann Arbor, MI 48109–1115

Internet Addresses

Convention on International Trade in Endangered Species
  http://www.wcmc.org.uk:80/CITES/english/index.html

EcoNet: Habitats and Species
  http://www.igc.apc.org/igc/issues/habitats

EE–Link: Endangered Species, University of Michigan
  http://www.nceet.snre.umich.edu/EndSpp/Endangered.html

Endangered Species Act (brief history), University of Oregon
  http://gladstone.uoregon.edu/~cait/

Endangered Species Home Page, U.S. Fish and Wildlife Service
  http://www.fws.gov/~r9endspp/endspp.html

Endangered Species Protection Program, U.S. Environmental
  Protection Agency
  http://www.epa.gov/espp

Endangered Species Study Web: General Resources
  http://www.studyweb.com/animals/endang/endanger.htm

Endangered Species Update, University of Michigan
  http://www.umich.edu/~esupdate/

EnviroLink: Largest online environmental information resource
  http://www.envirolink.org/

Environmental Organization Web Directory: Wildlife and endangered species focus
  http://www.webdirectory.com/Wildlife/General_
  Endangered_Species

IUCN Red List of Threatened Animals
  http://www.wcmc.org.uk/data/database/rl_anml_combo.html

IUCN Red List of Threatened Plants
  http://www.wcmc.org.uk/species/plants/plant_redlist.html

Society for the Protection of Endangered Species (group of endangered species–related weblinks)
  http://pubweb.ucdavis.edu/Documents/GWS/Envissues/
  EndSpes/speshome.htm

Terra's Endangered Species Tour (includes range maps)
  http://www.olcommerce.com/terra/endanger.html

Organizations Focusing on Endangered and Threatened Species (selected list)

African Wildlife Foundation
1717 Massachusetts Ave., NW
Washington, DC 20036
(202) 265–8393; Fax: (202) 265–2361
Internet: http://www.awf.org
Organization that works to craft and deliver creative solutions
for the long–term well–being of Africa's remarkable species
and habitats.

American Cetacean Society
P.O. Box 1319
San Pedro, CA 90733–0391
(310) 548–6279; Fax: (310) 548–6950
Internet: http://www.acsonline.org
Nonprofit organization that works in the areas of conservation, education, and research to protect marine mammals, especially whales, dolphins, and porpoises, and the oceans in
which they live.

Animal Welfare Institute
P.O. Box 3650
Washington, DC 20007
(202) 337–2332; Fax: (202) 338–9478
Organization active in the protection of endangered species,
among other issues, related to animal welfare.

Center for Marine Conservation, Inc.
1725 DeSales St., NW, Suite 500
Washington, DC 20036
(202) 429–5609; Fax: (202) 872–0619
Nonprofit organization dedicated to protecting marine
wildlife and their habitats and to conserving coastal and
ocean resources.

Center for Plant Conservation, Inc.
P.O. Box 299
St. Louis, MO 63166
(314) 577–9450; Fax: (314) 577–9465
Internet: http://www.mobot.org/CPC/
National network of 25 botanical gardens and arboreta dedi-
cated to the conservation and study of rare and endangered
U.S. plants.

The Conservation Agency
6 Swinburne Street
Jamestown, RI 02835
(401) 423–2652; Fax: (401) 423–2652
Organization that conducts research and gathers data specifically aimed to preserve rare, endangered, and little–known
species.

Defenders of Wildlife
  1101 14th St., NW, Suite 1400
  Washington, DC 20005
  (202) 682–9400; Fax: (202) 682–1331
  Internet: http://www.defenders.org/
  Nonprofit organization that works to protect and restore native species, habitats, ecosystems, and overall biological diversity.

Endangered Species Coalition
  666 Pennsylvania Ave., SE
  Washington, DC 20003
  (202) 547–9009
  Coalition of more than 200 organizations that seeks to broaden and mobilize public support for protecting endangered species.

International Union for Conservation of Nature and Natural Resources (IUCN–The World Conservation Union)
  U.S. Office: 1400 16th St., NW
  Washington, DC 20036
  (202) 797–5454; Fax: (202) 797–5461
  Internet: http://www.iucn.org
  An international independent body that promotes scientifically based action for the conservation of nature and for sustainable development. The Species Survival Commission (SSC) of the IUCN publishes biennial Red List books, which describe threatened species of mammals, birds, reptiles, amphibians, fish, invertebrates, and plants.

International Wildlife Coalition
  70 East Falmouth Highway
  East Falmouth, MA 02536
  (508) 548–8328; Fax: (508) 548–8542
  Internet: http://www.webcom.com/~iwcwww
  Nonprofit organization dedicated to preserving wildlife and their habitats. IWC's Whale Adoption Project preserves marine mammals.

International Wildlife Education and Conservation
  1140 Westwood Blvd., Suite 205
  Los Angeles, CA 90024
  (310) 208–3631; Fax: (310) 208–2779
  Internet: http://www.iwec.org/iwec.htm
  Nonprofit organization that seeks to ensure the future of endangered animals and to promote animal welfare through public education and conservation of habitats.

Marine Environmental Research Institute
  772 West End Ave.
  New York, NY 10025
  (212) 864–6285; Fax (212) 864–1470

Nonprofit organization dedicated to protecting the health and biodiversity of the marine environment, addressing such problems as global marine pollution, endangered species, and habitat destruction.

National Wildlife Federation
Laurel Ridge Conservation Education Center
8925 Leesburg Pike
Vienna, VA 22184–0001
(703) 790–4000; Fax: (703) 442–7332
Internet: http://www.nwf.org
Nonprofit organization that seeks to educate, inspire, and assist individuals and organizations of diverse cultures to conserve wildlife and other natural resources.

Nature Conservancy
1815 North Lynn St.
Arlington, VA 22209
(703) 841–5300; Fax: (703) 841–1283
Internet: http://www.tnc.org
International nonprofit organization committed to preserving biological diversity by protecting natural lands and the life they harbor.

Pacific Center for International Studies
33 University Sq., Suite 184
Madison, WI 53715
(608) 256–6312; Fax: (608) 257–0417
An international think tank specializing in the assessment of international treaty regimes, including the Convention on International Trade in Endangered Species (CITES) and the International Convention for the Regulation of Whaling (ICRW).

Save the Manatee Club
500 North Maitland Ave.
Maitland, FL 32751
(407) 539–0990; Fax: (407) 539–0871
Internet: http://www.objectlinks.com/manatee
National nonprofit organization that seeks to preserve the endangered West Indian manatee through public education, research funding, rescue, rehabilitation, and advocacy.

Wildlife Preservation Trust International, Inc.
3400 West Girard Ave.
Philadelphia, PA 19104
(215) 222–3636; Fax: (215) 222–2191
Organization that supports the preservation of endangered species through hands–on field work, research, education, and training.

World Conservation Monitoring Centre
219 Huntington Rd.
Cambridge, England CB3 0DL

(01223) 277314; Fax: (01223) 277136
Internet: http://www.wcmc.org.uk
Organization that supports conservation and sustainable development through the provision of information services on issues relating to nature conservation.

World Society for the Protection of Animals
29 Perkins St.
P.O. Box 190
Boston, MA 02130
(617) 522–7000; Fax: (617) 522–7077
International organization committed to the alleviation of animal suffering and to the conservation of endangered animals.

World Wildlife Fund
1250 24th St., NW
Washington, DC 20037
(202) 293–4800; Fax: (202) 293–9211
Internet: http://www.wwf.org
The largest private U.S. organization working worldwide to protect wildlife and wildlands—especially in the tropical forests of Latin America, Asia, and Africa.

Photo Credits

Photographs appearing in Endangered Species, *were received from the following sources:*

Photograph by Mark Boulton. Photo Researchers, Inc. Reproduced by permission: pp. 2, 58; **Photograph by Karl Weidmann. Photo Researchers, Inc. Reproduced by permission:** p. 5; **Photograph by Paul Crum. Photo Researchers, Inc. Reproduced by permission:** p. 8; **Photograph by Mike Dulaney. Cincinnati Zoo. Reproduced by permission:** p. 11; **Photograph by Jiri Lochman. Planet Earth Pictures Limited. Reproduced by permission:** p. 14; **Photograph by Merlin D. Tuttle. Photo Researchers, Inc. Reproduced by permission:** p. 16; **Photograph by Jeff Lepore. Photo Researchers, Inc. Reproduced by permission:** pp. 21, 177, 504; **Photograph by Tom McHugh. Photo Researchers, Inc. Reproduced by permission:** pp. 25, 49, 81, 87, 96, 130, 144, 165, 202, 205, 238, 275, 438, 445, 525, 528, 559, 562; **Photograph by Don W. Fawcett. Photo Researchers, Inc. Reproduced by permission:** p. 28; **Planet Earth Pictures Limited. Reproduced by permission:** pp. 32, 117, 149, 230, 364, 432; **Photograph by Renee Lynn. Photo Researchers, Inc. Reproduced by permission:** p. 35; **Photograph by S. R. Maglione. Photo Researchers, Inc. Reproduced by permission:** p. 38; **Photograph by Nigel J. Dennis. Photo Researchers, Inc. Reproduced by permission:** pp. 41, 53, 337; **Photograph by Stephen Dalton. Photo Researchers, Inc. Reproduced by permission:** p. 44; **Photograph by M. K. Ranjitsinh. Photo Researchers, Inc. Reproduced by permission:** p. 47; **Photograph by R. Dev. Photo Researchers, Inc. Reproduced by permission:** p. 62; **Photograph by Alan D. Carey. Photo Researchers, Inc. Reproduced by permission:** p. 66; **Photograph by Joseph Van Wormer. Photo Researchers, Inc. Reproduced by permission:** p. 71; **Photograph by Jerry L. Ferrara. Photo Re-**

searchers, Inc. Reproduced by permission: p. 74; **Cincinnati Zoo. Reproduced by permission:** pp. 78, 102, 111, 171, 280, 328, 415, 418, 519, 544; **San Diego Zoo, photograph by J. Gordon Miller. Reproduced by permission:** p. 84; **Photograph by Renee Lynn. Photo Researchers, Inc. Reproduced by permission:** p. 90; **Photograph by Susan Middleton. ©1998 Susan Middleton. Reproduced by permission:** p. 93; **Photograph by Gregory G. Dimijian. Photo Researchers, Inc. Reproduced by permission:** pp. 99, 108, 322; **Photograph by Douglas Faulkner. Photo Researchers, Inc. Reproduced by permission:** p. 105; **Photograph by Fletcher and Baylis. Photo Researchers, Inc. Reproduced by permission:** p. 114; **Photograph by Andrew L. Young. Photo Researchers, Inc. Reproduced by permission:** p. 120; **Photo Researchers, Inc. Reproduced by permission:** pp. 123, 181, 283, 367, 491, 568; **Photograph by Tim Davis. Photo Researchers, Inc. Reproduced by permission:** pp. 126, 233, 252, 553; **Photograph by Tim and Pat Leeson. Photo Researchers, Inc. Reproduced by permission:** pp. 135, 168, 198, 244, 301; **Photograph by Toni Angermayer. Photo Researchers, Inc. Reproduced by permission:** p. 139; **Photograph by M. Philip Kahl Jr. Photo Researchers, Inc. Reproduced by permission:** p. 152; **Photograph by Kenneth W. Fink. Photo Researchers, Inc. Reproduced by permission:** pp. 155, 226, 292; **Photograph by Numi C. Mitchell. The Conservation Agency. Reproduced by permission:** p. 159; **Photograph by Francois Gohier. Photo Researchers, Inc. Reproduced by permission:** pp. 162, 190, 556; **Photograph by Thor Janson. Photo Researchers, Inc. Reproduced by permission:** p. 174; **Photograph by Mitch Reardon. Photo Researchers, Inc. Reproduced by permission:** p. 184; **Photograph by Pieter Folkens. Planet Earth Pictures, Limited. Reproduced by permission:** p. 187; **Photograph by Myer Bornstein. Planet Earth Pictures Limited. Reproduced by permission:** p. 193; **Photograph by Leonard Lee Rue III. Photo Researchers, Inc. Reproduced by permission:** p. 208; **Photograph by Gilbert S. Grant. Photo Researchers, Inc. Reproduced by permission:** p. 218; **Photograph by R. and N. Bowers. Vireo. Reproduced by permission:** pp. 221, 236; **Photograph by R. Van Nostrand. Photo Re-**

searchers, Inc. Reproduced by permission: p. 241; **Photograph by Alain Evrard. Photo Researchers, Inc. Reproduced by permission:** p. 248; **Photograph by Karl W. Kenyon. Photo Researchers, Inc. Reproduced by permission:** p. 256; **Photograph by Dr. M. P. Kahl. Photo Researchers, Inc. Reproduced by permission:** p. 259; **Photograph by Roger Wilmshurst. Photo Researchers, Inc. Reproduced by permission:** p. 262; **Photograph by José Luis G. Grandé. Photo Researchers, Inc. Reproduced by permission:** p. 269; **Photograph by Jeanne White. Photo Researchers, Inc. Reproduced by permission:** p. 272; **Photograph by Nick Garbutt. Planet Earth Pictures, Limited. Reproduced by permission:** pp. 286, 550; **Photograph by E. R. Degginger. Photo Researchers, Inc. Reproduced by permission:** p. 289; **Photograph by Pete Oxford. Planet Earth Pictures, Limited. Reproduced by permission:** p. 295; **Photograph by R. L. Pitman. Vireo. Reproduced by permission:** p. 298; **Photograph by Lynx Edicions. Vireo. Reproduced by permission:** p. 305; **Photograph by Edmund Appel. Photo Researchers, Inc. Reproduced by permission:** p. 311; **Photograph by George Holton. Photo Researchers, Inc. Reproduced by permission:** p. 314; **Photograph by Bill Dyer. Photo Researchers, Inc. Reproduced by permission:** pp. 319, 341; **Photograph by Vincent Serventy. Planet Earth Pictures, Limited. Reproduced by permission:** p. 325; **Photograph by Doug Wechsler. Vireo. Reproduced by permission:** p. 331; **Photograph by S. and S. Rucker. Vireo. Reproduced by permission:** p. 334; **Photograph by Ken Lucas. Planet Earth Pictures, Limited. Reproduced by permission:** p. 344; **Photograph by David and Hayes Norris. Photo Researchers, Inc. Reproduced by permission:** pp. 347, 496; **©1994 Middleton/Littschwager. Reproduced by permission:** pp. 356, 359; **Photograph by Charles V. Angelo. Photo Researchers, Inc. Reproduced by permission:** p. 386; **Photograph by S. David Jenike. Cincinnati Zoo. Reproduced by permission:** p. 390; **Photograph by A. E. Spreitzer. All Rights Reserved. Reproduced by permission:** pp. 393, 396, 399, 409; **Photograph by Dr. Paula A. Zahl. Photo Researchers, Inc. Reproduced by permission:** pp. 412, 565; **Photograph by Charles E. Mohr. Photo Researchers,**

Index

Italic *type indicates volume numbers;* **boldface** *type indicates entries and their page numbers; (ill.) indicates illustrations.*

Venus's–flytrap *3: 505–07*, 506 (ill.)

Vermont (USA)
Cinquefoil, Robbins' *3:* 461
Mussel, dwarf wedge *2:* 391
Pogonia, small whorled *3:* 492

Vicugna vicugna 1: 180

Vicuña *1: 180–82*, 181 (ill.)

Vietnam
Bear, sun *1:* 24
Catfish, giant *3:* 428
Crocodile, saltwater *3:* 526
Deer, musk *1:* 46
Egret, Chinese *2:* 248
Elephant, Asian *1:* 61
Python, Indian *3:* 546
Tiger *1:* 176

Vireo atricapillus 2: 333

Vireo, black–capped *2: 333–35*, 334 (ill.)

Virginia (USA)
Bat, gray *1:* 15
Fanshell *2:* 388
Isopod, Madison Cave *2:* 354
Orchid, eastern prairie fringed *3:* 480
Pearlymussel, little–wing *2:* 397
Pogonia, small whorled *3:* 492
Spinymussel, James River *2:* 405

Virginia big–eared bat *1:* 19

Virginia spinymussel *2:* 406

Virgin Islands (British)
Conch, queen *2:* 384
Plover, piping *2:* 317

Virgin Islands (USA)
Conch, queen *2:* 384
Plover, piping *2:* 317

Volcano rabbit *1: 148–50*, 149 (ill.)

Vulture, California *2:* 225

Vulture, Cape *2: 336–39*, 337 (ill.)

W

Waldrapp *2:* 279

Wallaby, brindled nail–tailed *1: 183–85*, 184 (ill.)

Warbler, Kirtland's *2: 340–42*, 341 (ill.)

Washington (USA)
Albatross, short–tailed *2:* 216
Bear, grizzly *1:* 20
Murrelet, marbled *2:* 296
Owl, northern spotted *2:* 299
Sea lion, Stellar's *1:* 167

Weasel family *1:* 65, 132

Western lowland gorilla *1:* 75

Western Sahara
Cheetah *1:* 37
Gazelle, dama *1:* 70
Gull, Audouin's *2:* 267
Oryx, scimitar–horned *1:* 129

West Indian manatee *1: 104–06*, 105 (ill.)

West Virginia (USA)
Bat, Virginia big–eared *1:* 19
Spinymussel, James River *2:* 405

Wetapunga *2: 382–84*

Whale, blue *1: 186–88*, 187 (ill.)

Whale, humpback *1: 189–91*, 190 (ill.)

Whale, sulfur–bottomed *1:* 186

White–breasted thrasher *2: 330–32*, 331 (ill.)

Whooping crane *2: 232–34*, 233 (ill.)

Wild rice, Texas *3: 508–10*, 509 (ill.)

Wild water buffalo *1: 31–33*, 32 (ill.)

Wild yak *1: 204–06*, 205 (ill.)

Windward Islands
Conch, queen *2:* 384

Wisconsin (USA)
Dragonfly, Hine's emerald *2:* 375
Orchid, eastern prairie fringed *3:* 480

Wolf, African painted *1:* 52

Wolf, gray *1: 192–96*, 193 (ill.), 197

Wolf, red *1: 197–200*, 198 (ill.)

Wolf, strand *1:* 86

Wolf, timber *1:* 192

Wombat, Barnard's hairy–nosed *1:* 201

Wombat, northern hairy–nosed *1: 201–03*, 202 (ill.)

Wombat, Queensland hairy–nosed *1:* 201

Woodchuck *1:* 113

Woodpecker, ivory–billed *2: 343–45*, 344 (ill.)

Woodpecker, red–cockaded *2: 346–48*, 347 (ill.)

Woolly spider monkey *1: 119–21*, 120 (ill.), 142

Wyoming (USA)
Bear, grizzly *1:* 20
Ferret, black–footed *1:* 65
Toad, Wyoming *3:* 425

Wyoming toad *3: 426–28*, 427 (ill.)

Y

Yak, wild *1: 204–06*, 205 (ill.)

Yellow–eyed penguin *2: 313–15*, 314 (ill.)

Yellow–shouldered blackbird *2: 220–22*, 221 (ill.)

Yemen
Ibis, northern bald *2:* 278

Yugoslavia
Pelican, Dalmatian *2:* 309
Salmon, Danube *3:* 439
Sturgeon, Baltic *3:* 443

Z

Zambia
Cheetah *1:* 37
Dog, African wild *1:* 52
Elephant, African *1:* 57
Lovebird, black–cheeked *2:* 287
Rhinoceros, black *1:* 151

Zebra, Grevy's *1: 207–09*, 208 (ill.)

Zimbabwe
Cheetah *1:* 37
Dog, African wild *1:* 52
Elephant, African *1:* 57
Hyena, brown *1:* 86
Lovebird, black–cheeked *2:* 287
Rhinoceros, black *1:* 151
Vulture, Cape *2:* 335

Zizania texana 3: 508